Sensuous Cooking

Steve Urevith

KENDALL/HUNT PUBLISHING COMPANY
4050 Westmark Drive   Dubuque, Iowa 52002

This edition has been printed directly from camera-ready copy.

Copyright © 1994 by Steve Urevith

ISBN 0-8403-9479-9

Library of Congress Catalog Card Number: 94-76448

Printed in the United States of America
10 9 8 7 6 5 4 3 2 1

Table of Contents

Preface... 3

Foreword.. 4

Acknowledgments... 5

Introduction... 6

Chapter One - Old Sensualities 9

Chapter Two - Special Sensuousness.. 33

Chapter Three - Out of Town Sensuousness 63

Chapter Four - Sensuous People.. 84

Chapter Five - Sensuous Elegance.. 109

Chapter Six - Ethnic Sensuousness 126

Postscript.. 156

Preface

It is such an honor for me to write the foreword to Steve Urevith's book, "Sensuous Cooking". Not just because I believe in the recipes and the concept but because he is my brother.

When I think of "Sensuous Cooking" I imagine the aroma of the flavorings, the dash of color and of course the mood that the dinner creates. My brother and I certainly had our share of meals that appealed to the senses. I think of our mom's apple pie. So good, so succulent that years later all I have to do is close my eyes and I am back in her kitchen tasting a bite of still the best apple pie I ever had.

Unfortunately for my brother and I our parents died when I was 10 and Steve 18. Steve became brother, mother, father and yes, cook for me, his kid sister. His first dish, "Mustard Chicken" was certainly colorful and aromatic, but using Polish mustard sure put too much zest in it. We laughed over his blunder, but Steve improved and his art perfected. In fact, his dinners, lunches and breakfasts are always appealing. No matter what Steve makes, he always places his heart and soul into it.

And, heart and soul is what "Sensuous Cooking" is all about. It doesn't matter how much or how little money you have, you can still create a meal that will appeal to all your senses.

I hope you will enjoy not just the meals but the many anecdotes about growing up with my brother.

Foreword

    "Sensuous Cooking" is a book I wrote to heighten my readers' sensuality by cooking. This book does not have recipes that only world class chefs can make, but rather, it is for you the reader to make. The book is whimsical; I don't want my readers to follow my recipes verbatim, I want my readers to appreciate their efforts, to bathe in the light of their efforts in preparing a certain dish. I want my readers to have fun and be anxious-free in the kitchen. I feel that the recipes in this book should touch your senses. You should feel, see, hear the food you are making. You should fantasize about a setting or mood you want to create. Cook the dinner to please yourself and the person/persons you are cooking for. Prepare the dishes in an evening gown, tuxedo or naked. Have a picnic in your car or in the lobby of a theatre. Think of your favorite movie and create that scene at home. Cater a small office party with some of the recipes of "Sensuous Cooking".

    When I give ideas for a table setting, it is just an idea of mine. You set the table, always try a different mood for your table. Make your meals events. Live the recipes, crank up the music, polish the silverware, change your eating environment. This is a book to heighten and develop your sensuality towards cooking. "Sensuous Cooking" is devoted to setting a mood, casting a spell, and subtle seductiveness. It is you who are creating their mood and you are the most important person in the world.

Acknowledgments

I would like to thank the following people who have made this book a reality.

Sonia Schlener. My wife of 20 years, who always supported me and made me a better person than I was 20 years ago.

Patricia Urevith. My sister, who put up with me in my wild youth and who acted as a guinea pig for my early cooking experiments.

Steve and Peter Sclafani of Peter's Fish Market in Midland Park, New Jersey, who always supplied me with the freshest fish in the market and who put up with my endless blabber.

Al Runo of Kings Supermarket in Ridgewood, New Jersey, for having great produce and meats.

Terrance McCluskey of Hollywood Film Art for great photos.

Natalie Cohen of Just Your Type By Natalie for great word processing services.

Jill Nogrady for the wonderful covers she designed for "Sensuous Cooking".

Introduction

"Sensuous Cooking" is a book that basically traces my life, loves (lost and found) and feelings, with recipes as the focal point.

In my youth I was neither good-looking, sexy, articulate, or smart. When you look at it I was a nerd. Finding a girl to go out with was ofttimes impossible. I reached puberty in the late '50's and at that time my parents died, leaving me with an eight-years-younger sister and an apartment in Brooklyn. Growing up Polish and Russian in the '50's, food was an important part of life. I started to cook so that my sister would get a hot meal and I would have more to eat than just sandwiches.

I immediately started to love cooking and began amassing a pot and pan collection and a cookbook collection. I started to equate recipes with my feelings. The seasons were no longer a change in the weather, but a change in food supplies. Movies, theater, music all started to give me inspiration to make various dishes. Magazines, fictional characters and moods dictated the foods I was cooking, but nothing had such an effect on my recipes as the people I have met.

In the beginning it was cooking for my sister and making her happy with my dishes, then I became a real anomaly by cooking for various girlfriends. I am not saying my cooking transformed me into Paul Newman, but it was very unusual for a young man to cook the dinners.

My cooking as years went on became more sophisticated, along with dating. Then the ultimate partner came for my cooking. I met my wife, who has shared my life for twenty wonderful years. Cooking now has become a venture into love. When you are presenting dishes every day to someone who means so much to you, it is like each day giving a new gift to that person. Where a poem is a poem, and a painting is a painting, food is an everyday creation to the person in your life. After cooking for 31 years I love it more than ever.

The book "Sensuous Cooking" that I compiled is devoted to food and its wonderful sexy moods. Taste, smell, sight, touch and even hearing are involved with cooking. The right food barrages all the senses, awakens your insight, hits your brain in all directions. Food is an aphrodisiac, a mood maker, a strong seducer. Even the most rudimentary dates are centered on food. From teenagers holding hands in a fast food joint to an urban couple clinking wine glasses, food cushions you with a feeling of well-being.

In "Sensuous Cooking", I am taking a total approach to dining. I hate to think of a loving couple sitting by a TV eating microwaveable food or takeout. The recipes I have assembled are user-friendly and very romantic. They are meant to be savored, they are meant to prompt conversation, they are spark lighters and meant for lovers and loving people. They reach out to your sensuality and say "come".

The book hits on recipes that blend well with certain types of music. A certain dish says play this album on CD, the music will be heard as the food is tasted, then taste and sound will merge and two senses will be heightened. "Sensuous Cooking" also tries to set a mood with dishes and glassware. Everyone should own as many dishes and glasses as possible. Some dinnerware, like some food, becomes wearing; there should be a whimsicality in setting a table. Sensuality does not just mean black lace, it also means bright colors, offbeat patterns, soft hues or blaring trumpet designs. The patterns can be the obvious, or can be subtle.

Wake up in the morning, brush your teeth, go to work, but through all this have a reward for yourself. Make that reward dinner. Pick a mood and I am not just saying Chinese, French, or Italian, I am saying pick an abstract feeling based on love, the senses, the weather, someone you met, someone you talked to, fantasize a situation - make your home a geisha house or a farm or a chalet. Don't just have dinner, make it the highlight of your day. We spend so little time on this planet, and if you spend your meals just eating, you have missed one of the great joys of the day.

Even if you have your dinner by yourself you can make it into a party. For 13 years I lived alone, and a lot of it was lonely, but with a touch of imagination and a positive feeling, my dinners were a joy even if I wasn't sharing them with a lover, friend or associate.

Drink is very important to the total concept of Sensuous Cooking. The beverage you serve does not have to be a vintage wine, but it must be served as though the container was holding gold. Water, club soda, beer are all part of the total dining picture, and should not be taken for granted. Nothing in the portrait of your dining should be taken for granted. You are putting yourself in this package, you are saying: "This is me and this is what I am doing for you."

The food is presented, the beverage served, the music played, the table made, the glasses polished, the flatware picked, and you are composing a mood so that when you awake the next day you say to yourself, "Wow, that was an experience, did I do that? Did I accomplish this? I feel immersed in the art of pleasing my senses, my companions, my environment. I feel I just made the world a little better because of the little effort and care I took in making eating into a sensuous experience."

What my book is crying out for is not to leave a table with the meal having been good, the book wants you to leave a little breathless, a little pampered in the knowledge that cooking is an art of sensuality. Your cooking implements are your brushes and the table is your canvas, the foods are your paints, and instead of your creation just hitting your eyes, your creation has heightened all your senses.

As you can probably tell, cooking means a lot in my life. It is my way of offering myself to a person. I feel my life has become better, and I have become a better person, through my cooking. My everyday life is not humdrum, nor is it glamorous, romantic or adventuresome; however, when I come home at night with game plan in mind for the evening fare, I feel like I am a great seducer, or painter, or musician, all of which I am not. But with the notion of cooking sensuously I am transported to a place in my mind where I want to be: A beach, a play, or on a rolling wagon of passion.

Finally, I would like to dedicate this book to the two most important people in my life: my wife Sonia, my life of 20 years, who has taught me to love; and my sister Pattie, who always tries for me.

Chapter One

Old Sensualities

The following are recipes that have always seemed to be there. No one really knows where they came from; but, they have been made, with variations, for years. To appreciate and understand what we have today, we should reflect on yesterday. Our civilization has been built stone upon stone, and so have our identities and personas been so built. I love making these old classics, they bring memories, they make me think and ponder of an era that has passed. The recipes in this chapter should take you through time to remember your first day at school, the time you sneaked a smoke, your first date, your first lover. Even if the thoughts you get are not pleasant, you can change them, learn from mistakes you made, vow to be that better person.

When I think of some of these recipes, I actually feel a comfortable place in time. These recipes were for their time elegant dishes, they were served in restaurants and at parties. The dishes were made, pre high fiber diet, and pre cholesterol, and the pre "What mutual fund should I buy" era. These were recipes that were served at home on a Sunday afternoon or in your favorite restaurant. This chapter is to give to you the sensuousness of the past.

Coq Au Vin

Sensuousness

These recipes bring to mind memories of long past. If you can associate parts of your past with food as I do they conjure up good memories. Have you ever been to a place and there is a smell and you say: "It makes me think of school or it makes me think of my parents or it makes me think of a home I once lived in"? Well recipes do that for me and if you are sensuous enough they can conjure up memories of sensuality. I had Coq Au Vin when I was about 8 years old. My parents took me to a French restaurant whose name I cannot remember now and I feel I have duplicated this dish.

Ingredients

1 chicken, cut into serving pieces

6 slices bacon

6 pearly onions

1 lb mushrooms, sliced

4 carrots, halved

1 cup chicken broth

1 cup red wine

1/4 cup flour

1 tsp salt

1 tsp freshly ground pepper

2 cloves garlic, minced

1/4 tsp thyme

2 bay leaves

Preparation

Coat chicken in mixture of flour, salt, and pepper. Fry bacon in Dutch oven until crisp. Remove bacon. Brown chicken in bacon drippings. Remove. Saute onions and mushrooms until onions are tender. Remove. Drain off all fat. Stir in all the other ingredients. Stir crumbled bacon bits on top. Simmer 1 1/2 hours.

Table Setting

As French as possible, white plates, black silverware

Beverage

I feel not to be redundant, because red wine is in Coq Au Vin, I would make the drink of choice a French beer, France does have great beers!

Music

Bizet; I love Carmen with Coq Au Vin. People who don't like opera can be stirred very much to Carmen.

Steak au Poivre

Sensuousness

This recipe takes me way way back. This is an underrated recipe, and with steak coming back into prominence it should be gastronomically correct. Steak is so robust, especially if it's done well.

Ingredients

1 1/4 lb boneless sirloin steak

4 Tbls crushed black peppercorns

2 tsps salt

1/4 cup red wine

Preparation

Crush peppercorns vigorously and press into the steak. Let steak stand at room temperature for 1 hour. Heat a heavy skillet until very hot. Put a piece of fat from the steak into the skillet. Sear the steak on both sides. Reduce heat and cook 3 mins. on each side. Remove steak. Sprinkle with salt. Add wine to skillet, stirring constantly, for 1 min. Pour wine sauce over steak.

Accompaniment
French fried potatoes

Table Setting
Platters go well with this and a side board of a Caesar's Salad as well

Beverage
Muscadet wine

Music
Songs of The Left Bank

Chicken Curry

Sensuousness

A curry is really a non-existent spice; what it is is a conglomeration of different spices. When you cook with curry, your whole house will feel this dish. This is not a private dish.

Ingredients

1 - 2 1/2 lb broiler chicken, cut up

2 tsps salt

3 Tbls corn oil

1 large onion, coarsely chopped

3 cloves garlic, minced

1 - 6 oz can tomato paste

1 cup water

4 Tbls curry powder

1 tsp sugar

1 cup unflavored yogurt

1/2 cup sour cream

Preparation

Sprinkle chicken with salt. Brown in hot oil in a heavy Dutch oven. Add onion and garlic. Cook until onion is wilted. Pour off the fat. Combine tomato paste, water, curry, sugar. Pour over chicken. Simmer, covered, 45 mins. Blend yogurt and sour cream. Remove chicken from heat and blend in yogurt and sour cream over very low heat. Do not let it boil.

Accompaniment
Bahaini rice

Table Setting
The table setting should be Indian - bright reds and gold should be used

Beverage
Cold Indian beer

Music
Theme from Passage To India

Veal Parmesan

Sensuousness

You must say to yourself "Why buy a cookbook that has Veal Parmesan as a recipe?" Well this Veal Parmesan comes from a great restaurant in Greenwich Village in New York City. Bring lots of money. They make Veal Parmesan like no place ever can. This is as close as I can get to their recipe. The recipe is for two people.

Ingredients

2 veal chops*

2 eggs, lightly beaten

1 cup Italian flavored bread crumbs

1/2 cup olive oil

1 can - 8 oz tomato sauce

1/2 lb fresh mozzarella

1/4 lb grated Parmesan

*Pound the meat very, very thin; crack the bone and pound the bone until very, very thin

Preparation

Dip the veal chops/cutlets into egg and then into the bread crumbs. Saute in hot olive oil in heavy frying pan until golden on each side. Put cutlets on a baking dish. Pour tomato sauce over each. Sprinkle with Parmesan. Top with mozzarella and bake in a preheated 375º oven for 20 mins.

Accompaniment   Shaved Truffles

Table Setting   However you feel

Beverage   Black Velvets

Music   Leontyne Price

Sherried Chicken with Green Noodles

Sensuousness

This again goes way back to my youth and isn't it funny, I wonder if you, who are reading my book are thinking of dishes and places you've been in your life. This is a dish that I had on probably one of my first dates, at a restaurant called Toffinetti's in Times Square in New York which since became a Nathan's and which since has closed down.

Ingredients

1 broiler/fryer chicken, cut up into serving pieces

3 cups chicken broth

6 Tbls butter

6 Tbls flour

*Saute mushrooms briefly in butter

1 tsp paprika

1/4 cup sherry

1/2 lb mushrooms, thinly sliced*

Preparation

Place chicken in a heavy kettle. Cover with broth. Bring to the boil. Reduce heat. Simmer, covered, 40 mins. Remove chicken. Strain broth. Return broth to a boil. In a saucepan, melt 6 Tbls of butter. Add the flour and stir with a whisk until blended. Add the boiling broth all at once, stirring vigorously with the whisk until the sauce is thickened and smooth. Season with salt and stir in the sherry. Remove meat from the chicken. Add the chicken and mushrooms to the sauce and serve over green noodles.

Accompaniment
Peas

Table Setting
Casual, dress down for this, this is a dish that is to be enjoyed in the most casual sense, even to be eaten with bathrobes

Beverage
Drink something '50's with this, martinis in martini glasses

Music
Beatles, Revolver

Chicken Fricassee

Sensuousness

This dish is a soul soothing recipe dating back to the '30's and is now again becoming quite fashionable. I made this dish a long time ago on one of my first dates and I have made it since through the years.

Ingredients

1 - 3 lb broiler/fryer chicken, cut up	3 Tbls butter
3 cups water	3 Tbls flour
1 carrot, sliced	1 tsp salt
1 small onion, sliced	1 cup heavy cream
4 peppercorns	

Preparation

Place the chicken in a pot and add the water, carrot, onion, and bring to the boiling point. Simmer the chicken about 1 hour and 20 mins. Add the peppercorns after 45 mins. Remove chicken to a platter. In a saucepan, melt the butter. Combine with the flour. Pour into the chicken stock. Stir in the cream and stir until thickened. Do not boil. Return chicken and serve with the sauce.

Accompaniment
Mashed potatoes and peas

Table Setting
'50's, perhaps a toy '50's refrigerator as a centerpiece

Beverage
Schaefer Beer

Music
Dion and The Belmonts

Brunswick Stew

Sensuousness

This is Southern cooking at its best. You can picture yourself on a very warm, sunny day in Mississippi or Alabama. Dress as frivolously as possible for this Brunswick Stew. This is another dish that would go very well on a picnic or an outing and to be shared with somebody you love of course. As a matter of fact all food in my book should be shared by somebody you love and care about, including to be shared with yourself.

Ingredients

2 1/2 lb broiler/fryer chicken, quartered	4 med potatoes, diced
2 lbs pork spare ribs	1 cup green beans
1 1/2 quarts cold water	1 cup lima beans
1 Tbls salt	3 ears corn with the kernels off
1 tsp black peppercorns	7 fresh tomatoes, diced
1 tsp cayenne pepper	1 tsp freshly ground black pepper
1 small green pepper, diced	1 Tbls butter
1 med onion, diced	1 cup dry red wine

Preparation

Wash chicken and dry. Place in kettle with the spare ribs, salt, peppercorns, and cayenne. Cover with water and simmer 3 hours until the meat falls off the bones. Remove chicken and ribs. Cut the chicken and ribs into cubes, discarding the bones. Return to stock. Add vegetables, pepper, butter, and wine. Cover and simmer again 1 hour, stirring frequently.

Accompaniment

A bowl of dirty rice

Table Setting

To be eaten outdoors on a bright sunny day with a checkered tablecloth and even plastic wine glasses

Beverage

Iced Tea

Music

Theme from Song of the South

Oxtail Stew

Sensuousness

Oxtail Stew goes to my roots. One of the first dishes I made over 27 years ago. Oxtails at that time were literally given away. Today, upper class restaurants have discovered them and what they have been doing is boiling the meat off the bones and making it into various molds. Oxtail meat is very hearty, very delicate, and very let yourself go.

Ingredients

2 lbs oxtails, cut into 2 inch pieces

1/4 cup flour

3 Tbls corn oil

1 tsp salt

1 tsp ground pepper

2 med onions, sliced

2 cloves garlic, crushed

1 can - 35 oz Italian tomatoes

1 bay leaf

1 tsp dried basil

4 med potatoes, quartered

3 ribs celery, cut in 1 inch pieces

3 carrots, cut in 1 inch pieces

Preparation

Coat oxtails in flour. Fry in oil in a heavy Dutch oven until golden. Remove and sprinkle with salt and pepper. Combine onions and garlic. Saute until tender. Stir in tomatoes, salt, bay leaf, and basil. Bring to the boil. Return oxtails and simmer, covered, 2 hours. Add vegetables. Return cover and simmer another hour.

Accompaniment

The stew has everything that you would need in it for a fine dinner.

Table Setting

Barnyard

Beverage

Thunderbird wine

Music

Janis Joplin

Veal Scallopine Marsala

Sensuousness

Marsala wine has a very, very special effect on the senses. Marsala, when added to Zabaglione, which is a must for this custard, gives the body a warm feeling. In Veal Scallopine Marsala, the same warmth is given from the Marsala wine, except a little bit more subtly. After an hour or an hour and a half of eating this dish a warm feeling comes over you and then take it from there.

Ingredients

1 lb veal cutlets, sliced thin	1/4 lb sweet butter
1/4 cup flour	1/4 cup Marsala wine
1 tsp salt	1/2 cup water
1 tsp white pepper	2 pimentos, chopped
1 tsp oregano	2 tsps olive oil

Preparation

Cut veal into bite sized pieces. Combine flour, salt, white pepper, oregano, and dust each piece of veal using all the flour mixture. Melt butter and oil in heavy frying pan and brown veal for about 4 mins. on each side, covered. Add water, wine, pimentos. Stir very well and simmer for 5 mins.

Accompaniment

Very small boiled potatoes or potato croquettes and fried escarole

Table Setting

Should reflect warmth, bright candlelight, dark, dim lights, black plates, silverware

Beverage

Asti Spumonte

Music

Tito Puente

Swiss Steak Family Style

Sensuousness

When I was single I obviously didn't have much family except for my sister and my friend Larry. Larry just seemed to have melted into a Californian. He may have been mistaken for a phony; but, Larry was real in a surreal sense. To cook for a friend is also a sensuous experience.

Ingredients

2 lbs beef chuck, 2 inches thick

1/4 cup sherry wine vinegar

1/4 cup sherry

2 Tbls bouillon

1 clove garlic, minced

Dash of Tabasco sauce

2 Tbls corn oil

1 small onion, chopped

1/2 cup water

1/2 cup chili sauce

2 tomatoes, peeled, seeded, and quartered

Preparation

Marinate meat in sherry vinegar, sherry wine, bouillon, garlic, and Tabasco overnight, turning occasionally. Drain meat and reserve marinade. Brown meat well on both sides in hot oil in heavy casserole. Add marinade, onion, water, and chili sauce. Cover and simmer 1 hour and 15 mins. Add tomatoes and heat through.

Accompaniment
Mashed potatoes on the lumpy side

Table Setting
As family as possible with big serving pieces and streamers from the chandelier

Beverage
Tequila and salt, Larry's favorite drink

Music
Neil Diamond's Hot August Night

Chili Con Carne

Sensuousness

The debate over chili is unrelenting; to beans or not to beans, that seems to be the important question, but back in the '60's when we didn't know from the 5,000 different chilis that were there, Chili Con Carne was on every menu in just about every restaurant. It is a dish where only the fanciful and whimisical need apply. Have a blast with this dish..

Ingredients

1 lb ground round

2 med onions, chopped

1 - 17 oz can plum tomatoes

1 - 1 lb can kidney beans, drained

8 oz tomato sauce

2 Tbls corn oil

1 tsp sugar

3 Tbls chili powder

1/4 tsp cayenne

1 Tbls salt

Preparation

Brown onions and beef in hot oil in heavy casserole. Drain fat. Stir in tomatoes, liquid from beans, tomato sauce, and seasoning. Simmer, uncovered, for 1 hour. Add beans and simmer 15 mins. more, uncovered.

Accompaniment

Rice and cactus salsa

Table Setting

Try to get as close to Tex Mex as possible, cactus, dried flowers, toss in some tumbleweed in your dining room

Beverage

Lone Star Beer

Music

Theme from the 1963 movie The Alamo with John Wayne, Frankie Avalon, etc.

Trout Grenoble

Sensuousness

I once knew a person who I admired and no longer see. She was a vegetarian and back in the '60's or '50's meat was very popular. This recipe takes you back to a more romantic period than you may be in today and Trout Grenoble was my concession to a non-meat eater.

Ingredients

2 med sized trout

8 mushrooms, minced

3 Tbls bread crumbs

Juice of 1 lemon

5 Tbls butter

2 Tbls capers

1/4 cup flour

Dash salt

Dash white pepper

Preparation

Wash and clean trout. Dip trout in mixture of flour, salt, and pepper. Heat 2 Tbls of butter in heavy frying pan and brown trout on both sides. Remove trout and keep warm. In same pan, add remaining butter and saute the mushrooms with the bread crumbs for 4 mins. Add the lemon juice and capers and stir briskly. Pour over trout and serve.

Accompaniment

Boiled potatoes with dill and parsley

Table Setting

Setting with a basket of vegetables and fruit, picture of Van Gogh portraits in the dining room, glass plates

Beverage

Dry white Chablis

Music

Harper's Bizarre

Chicken à la King

Sensuousness

You are saying, "In Sensuous Cooking, Chicken à la King." Again Sensuous Cooking is to take you back in time so you can remember the senses that the food ticks a certain feeling on you. Chicken à la King, I made with one of my last "women friends" before I married Sonia. Her name is Jan and she was a very special person, and I still think she is a very special person, and when I think of Chicken à la King, I think of her and I think back to my childhood and I think back to various lunches and dinners I had with friends and business associates and relatives.

Ingredients

8 oz mushrooms, sliced

1/2 cup diced green pepper

1/2 cup butter

1/4 cup flour

1 tsp salt

1 tsp white pepper

2 cups chicken stock

2 cups light cream

1 lb cooked chicken breasts, cubed

1 jar - 4 oz pimentos, chopped

2 tsps paprika

Preparation

Cook mushrooms and green pepper in butter in a medium heavy skillet over medium heat. Remove from heat. Blend in flour, salt, pepper. Cook, stirring, over low heat until bubbly. Remove from heat. Stir in broth and cream. Heat to boiling, stirring constantly. Boil 1 min. Add chicken and pimento. Heat through. Put in tureen and top with paprika.

Accompaniment
Boiled potatoes and new peas

Table Setting
1950's if you can get it, pictures of James Dean, Marilyn Monroe

Beverage
Hoffman Ginger Ale

Music
Sha Na Na

Burgundy Beef

Sensuousness

Burgundy Beef is also called Beef Bourguignon. It is a common dish in French restaurants. It goes back many, many years and I have shared this dish with many lovers and dates and always felt a little better after sharing this dish with my potential lovers.

Ingredients

1 med onion, sliced

1 bay leaf

1/4 tsp rosemary

1 cup Burgundy wine

1 Tbls red wine vinegar

1 Tbls peanut oil

1 1/2 lbs rump steak, cut into 2 inch pieces

1/4 lb salt pork, finely diced

3/4 lb small whole mushrooms

1 cup beef broth

2 Tbls flour dissolved in 1/4 cup water

Preparation

Combine onion, bay leaf, rosemary, and oil in a large bowl. Add the meat. Marinate for 1 hour. Drain. Reserve marinade. Fry salt pork over medium heat in a heavy Dutch oven. Add meat, onion, and mushrooms. Cook until onion is tender, about 6 mins. Stir in the beef broth and marinade. Cover. Bring to boil. Reduce heat. Simmer 1 hour. Remove. Simmer another 1/2 hour. Add the flour and water paste to the mixture. Stir until sauce thickens, cooking slowly. Cook over low heat stirring constantly for 1 min.

Accompaniment

New potatoes with parsley and butter

Table Setting

The setting should have flowers, large wine goblets and your best china

Beverage

A lot of people would say this is redundant, however, I feel Burgundy wine goes very well with this beef

Music

101 Strings playing various songs

Chicken Cacciatore

Sensuousness

This is a very basic dish that adds to the grandeur of your senses. I made Chicken Cacciatore for the first time about 27 years ago, and I have made it ever since. It is not a "neat" dish but it is one that makes you aware of the little things. It has lustiness and heartiness to it. It is a dish uncommon today on most Italian menus.

Ingredients

1 broiler/fryer chicken, cut up into serving pieces

1 med onion, chopped

1 clove garlic, chopped

1/4 cup olive oil

1 tsp dried basil

1/4 cup dry sherry

17 oz can imported tomatoes

1 tsp salt

1 tsp freshly ground pepper

Preparation

Brown chicken in hot oil until lightly golden. Add onions and garlic and brown chicken well on all sides for about 8 mins. Add basil. Add the wine a little at a time until it evaporates. Add tomatoes, salt, and pepper. Blend well. Cover and simmer for 40 mins.

Accompaniment

A big platter of pasta

Table Setting

This is a dish that should be doubled or tripled in the ingredients. A big platter and dainty glasses

Beverage

Chianti wine

Music

Tony Bennett

Pot Au Feu

Sensuousness

Pot Au Feu is the French version of the New England boiled dinner. This is a dish I had many times in France and it is hearty, robust, and lively. Instead of having your in-laws or your mother and father over for a New England boiled dinner, make them a Pot Au Feu.

Ingredients

3 lbs rump of beef

1 piece cracked veal knuckle

1 piece shin bone

4 quarts water

4 carrots, sliced

2 med white turnips, peeled and sliced

6 leeks, washed and sliced

5 large potatoes, whole

1 large onion, whole

5 sprigs parsley

2 Tbls salt

5 whole black peppercorns

4 whole cloves

1 bay leaf

1 tsp dried thyme

Preparation

In a large heavy Dutch oven put meat and bones, water, salt, and peppercorns. Simmer for 2 1/4 hours, skimming the fat frequently. Add the vegetables and herbs. Simmer another 1 1/2 hours. Put meat on platter. Decorate with the vegetables and slice against the grain.

Accompaniment

All the vegetables are here; this is a full one pot dinner

Table Setting

Murals of Paris or travel posters in your dining room

Beverage

Rich Cabernet Sauvignon

Music

Music from Can Can

Hungarian Goulash

Sensuousness

Hungary is a romantic country unto itself. The doors of Hungary are Gypsies, caravans, fortune tellers, hardiness, ruggedness. Hungarian cuisine is much overlooked in this country and this is a basic recipe. It goes back years and years and years, and again, the basic recipes have the most sensuousness to them.

Ingredients

1 1/2 lbs boneless chuck, cut into cubes

3 large onions, thinly sliced

3 Tbls fat from the chuck

3 tsps Hungarian Paprika

1 tsp salt

1 tsp ground black pepper

Dash cayenne

1 bay leaf

1/2 cup water

1/2 cup sour cream

Preparation

Saute onions in hot fat in Dutch oven about 10 mins. Remove. Brown meat over medium heat in remaining fat. Add paprika, salt, pepper, cayenne. Return onions, bay leaf, and water. Cover and bring to a boil. Reduce heat and simmer 1 hour. Remove from heat and fold in sour cream.

Accompaniment
Buttered noodles

Table Setting
Christmas type tablecloth, wooden spoons and forks. The serving utensils should be wood.

Beverage
Hungarian red wine

Music
Tschaichovsky's Violin Concerto

Flank Steak Roulade

Sensuousness

A lot of these recipes, as you can probably tell by the ingredients, go back to the beginnings of my cooking. Steak was very big in the '50's and '60's and is now coming back in the 90's. Today's cuts are much leaner although, alas, not as tasty as they were back in the '50's and '60's. Flank steak was not a very popular cut back when I started cooking, it was unique and is probably my favorite cut of steak.

Ingredients

1/2 cup chopped onion	2 lbs flank steak
1/2 cup chopped green pepper	1 Tbls corn oil
6 Tbls butter	2 cups Italian canned tomatoes
3 cups beef broth	1 tsp dried basil
3 cups cooked rice	

Preparation

Saute onion and pepper in butter. Add rice and beef broth. Pound steak with a couple of teaspoons of beef broth on both sides. Spread about 1 cup of rice mixture on steak. Roll up and secure with string. Brown steak in hot oil. Add tomatoes, basil, and remaining beef broth. Simmer 1 1/2 hours. Remove cover and simmer 15 more minutes.

Accompaniment

A mixture of kale and potatoes, also known as Colcannon, goes marvelously with this. You have your rice already. Fresh green peas go well, and I like celery root with steak dishes.

Table Setting

Quiet, again, this dish is to be shared; no friends for this dish, just you and your lover.

Beverage

Gallo Burgundy

Music

Quiet, maybe a little light jazz like George Benson

Country Captain

Sensuousness

The sensuousness of country is deeply rooted in its origins. This is a traditional Southern dish. The scene that should be set is man in white suit, woman in flowing gown. It is to be eaten on a bright sunny summer day out of doors.

Ingredients

1 broiler/fryer chicken, cut into serving pieces

1/2 cup unsifted flour

2 tsps salt

1 tsp white pepper

3 Tbls corn oil

1 large onion, finely chopped

1 large green pepper, finely chopped

2 cloves garlic

2 Tbls curry powder

1 lb can of imported Italian tomatoes

1/2 cup golden raisins

Preparation

Combine flour and salt in a plastic bag. Place chicken in said bag and shake to evenly coat. Heat oil in a heavy Dutch oven casserole. Place chicken in casserole a few pieces at a time and brown. Remove chicken and keep warm. Add onion, pepper, garlic, and curry powder to the pan drippings. Saute until tender. Add the tomatoes, breaking them up with a fork. Add raisins. Return chicken to pan. Cover and simmer 1 hour.

Table Setting

This dish should be taken on a picnic where there might be an old mansion on the picnic grounds. A checkered plastic tablecloth, no candles for this dish, lots of paper towels, exchange greasy hands.

Beverage

Mint Julep and iced tea

Music

Blue Grass

28

Pepper Steak

Sensuousness

Chinese dining in the 1960's was Pepper Steak. Pepper Steak is such a basic dish but yet one that is overlooked in real good cooking. It is a dish that could be either very good or very bad, but, again, it is a dish that is significant of a culinary era that has gone by.

Ingredients

1 1/2 lbs round steak, cut into strips

1/2 cup chicken broth

1 Tbls garlic powder

3 Tbls light soy sauce

1 large onion, chopped

12 oz mushrooms, sliced

1 Tbls sugar

1/8 tsp pepper

1 Tbls flour dissolved in 2 Tbls water to make a paste

2 large green peppers, cut into strips

Preparation

Brown steak in the fatty pieces of steak. Remove. Pour broth and garlic into the wok. Simmer 5 mins. Stir in onion, soy sauce, mushrooms, sugar, and pepper. Stir in flour paste. Add meat. Cover and simmer 20 mins., stirring occasionally. Add green peppers. Remove cover and simmer 10 mins. more.

Table Setting

Reflecting the '50's and '60's. Be a little silly, a Chinese hat, pictures of Coney Island or places that you remember in the '50's and '60's. Think of your first Chinese experience, whether it be Chop Suey or Chow Mein. Reflect on how far Chinese cooking has come and appreciate the cuisine that it has brought to the United States.

Beverage

Tsing Tsao Beer

Music

The Platters

Veal Cordon Bleu

Sensuousness

My first experience in a French restaurant was in 1970 with a woman who was about 15 years older than me. It was a restaurant called The French Shack in New York City on, I believe, East 52nd Street. The woman is no longer a part of my life, but in moments I think about her and what it would have been like to have been with her for the rest of my life. This is a dish that was elegant back in the early '70's but now has sort of taken the stance of Lobster Thermidor or Veal Scaloppine or other dishes of the '50's and '60's. It is a dish that reminds me of a person and maybe it will take you back to the '50's, '60's, '70's.

Ingredients

6 veal cutlets	1 egg white
3 slices Swiss cheese	1/2 cup flour
3 slices Prosciutto	1 cup unseasoned bread crumbs
3 Tbls Dijon mustard	6 Tbls butter

Preparation

Spread 3 cutlets with mustard. Add slices of Prosciutto and cheese on each cutlet. Cover with remaining cutlets. Seal edges with a little egg white. Dredge in flour, then egg white, then bread crumbs. Saute very gently in melted butter in a medium heavy pan for 3 - 5 mins. on each side.

Table Setting

A '50's atmosphere - a picture of James Dean on the dining room wall. Dress with slicked back hair, maybe a polyester sports coat. For a woman, pedal pushers, or maybe a black dress with white pearls.

Beverage

Sauternes

Music

Elvis Presley

Cornish Game Hen

Sensuousness

What do you do on a spring afternoon? The temperature is 70 degrees, it feels good, the first blush of spring after a long winter. The recipe calls for something not different, not unusual, but something to usher in a new season. This appeals to that feeling you know of when that first warmth comes after a winter. This is my recipe dedicated to that. The serving is for two.

Ingredients

1 Cornish game hen, split in half

3/4 lb mushrooms, finely sliced

1 med onion, sliced

3 Tbls butter

1 cup chicken stock

1/2 cup white wine

1 tsp garlic salt

1 tsp poultry seasoning

Preparation

Heat butter in heavy skillet. Brown hen halves on both sides and remove. Add mushrooms and onions to pan. Saute until brown. Add wine and broth. Return hen halves to skillet. Cover and simmer 1 hour.

Table Setting

Should usher in the spring - bright lights, turn on all the lights in the dining room. Eat with colored forks, colored plates, colored glasses.

Beverage

Iced Tea

Music

Vivaldi's 4 Seasons

Beef Neapolitano

Sensuousness

I once saw a movie with Marlon Brando and Jean Simmons called Desiree, and I wondered what it would be like to live in the Napoleonic age, what did Napoleon try to do to be romantic with his woman? If he were a cook, what would he cook? And this is the recipe I would cook if I were cooking for Desiree.

Ingredients

1 lb boneless beef chuck

2 Tbls flour

1 can tomato paste

Juice of 1/4 lemon

1 tsp dried oregano

1 tsp garlic powder

1 tsp sugar

1 tsp freshly ground black pepper

3/4 lb fresh cut green beans

12 pearly onions

Preparation

Dredge meat in flour. Brown well on both sides in a heavy cast iron skillet. Add rest of ingredients except beans and onions, stir well. Simmer 1 1/2 hours. Stir in the beans and onions. Simmer 15 mins.

Table Setting

Gargantuan, larger than life, large candelabra, large, oversized plates, oversized utensils, pretty loud lighting

Beverage

Red wine and French brandy mixed

Music

Soundtrack from the silent film Napoleon

Chapter Two

Special Sensuousness

The following recipes are designed for that special occasion day. There are your standard days: birthday, Valentine's Day, Christmas; but why not pick a day and celebrate it. My wife and I have chosen our anniversary date and we celebrate it, each month. On that day, the 26th of each month we give each other little treats and I make extra special foods. Sonia and I also celebrate/observe Passover, Christmas, Russian Christmas and Easter. On Saint Patrick's Day (we are not Irish) we eat Irish food. We try and get as many heritages of different people into our lives. My wife is Norwegian so we celebrate the 17th of May, Norwegian Independence Day. On the 17th of May we have gjetost, herring, and liver postei. On Cinco de Mayo we have Mexican food and so on. Why should our senses just be limited to our origin? One of the beauties of food is that it is universal and we can learn so much of a culture through its foods and rituals of eating.

The recipes that follow are not necessarily ethnic but are good for a day that you wish to make special.

Valentine's Day Omelet

Sensuousness

I have been married for 20 happy years, and I have never celebrated Valentine's Day. I feel the purpose of it is to make card companies wealthy. Everyday to me is Valentine's Day because my love for my dear Sonia just grows stronger and stronger. Every day tell your lover "I love you", "I care about you" and "I live for you", then you'll have a Valentine's Day everyday.

Ingredients

4 eggs, well beaten

5 large mushrooms, sliced

3 slices cheddar cheese

3 Tbls butter

Pinch of dill

Pinch of tarragon

Pinch of white pepper

Preparation

In an omelet pan, saute mushrooms in 1 Tbl of butter. Add herbs and pepper to eggs. Beat well. Fold in the mushrooms. In the same omelet pan, heat the remaining butter. Add eggs and mushroom combination and pour to spread evenly over pan. Arrange cheese on top. When heated through fold omelet in half. Flip and allow to cook 1 min.

Accompaniment

Duchess potatoes goes real well with this

Table Setting

To be eaten in bed on a bed stand

Beverage

Mimosa

Music

Theme from Pal Joey, especially My Funny Valentine

Spring Chicken

Sensuousness

Spring to me has always been the most romantic time of the year. Spring, with that first blush of warm temperatures after 3 months of hard winter, warms up romances. This is a dish I made in honor to the rites of Spring.

Ingredients

1 broiler/fryer chicken, cut into serving pieces

3 Tbls butter

1 bunch scallions, cut up

1 lb mushrooms, sliced

17 oz can imported plum tomatoes, broken up

1 tsp salt

1 tsp pepper

3 Tbls finely chopped fresh dill

Preparation

Rinse and dry chicken. Sprinkle with salt and pepper. Heat butter in heavy skillet and cook chicken until brown on all sides. Remove and keep warm. Saute mushrooms and scallions for 5 mins. Add tomatoes, dill, salt, and pepper. Put chicken back in skillet and mix with tomato mixture. Cover and simmer 40 mins.

Accompaniment

Spring vegetables, cucumbers, a salad, and new potatoes

Table Setting

This dish I feel should be eaten outdoors on a picnic table

Beverage

May wine

Music

Music from Evita

Chicken with Paprika Rice

Sensuousness

This is a dish that would probably be mistaken for Chicken Paprish but there is a difference here, I created this dish when I was in a very Hungarian mood. I met a very, very charming couple who were from Hungary who had an influence on me and I cooked this for their pleasure.

Ingredients

2 Tbls corn oil

1 broiler/fryer, cut up

1 lb Hungarian sausage, sliced

6 scallions, chopped

2 green peppers, coarsely chopped

2 cloves garlic, coarsely chopped

3 whole tomatoes, peeled, seeded, and chopped

1 Tbls salt

1 Tbls Hungarian paprika

2 cups chicken stock

1 cup dry white wine

1 1/2 cups long grain rice

1/2 cup chopped parsley

Preparation

Brown chicken in oil. Remove. Brown sausages in same heavy casserole. Remove. Saute scallions and peppers about 8 mins. Add garlic, tomatoes, paprika, and salt. Stir in wine and chicken stock. Return chicken and cover. Simmer 25 mins. Return Hungarian sausage and rice. Simmer, covered, 20 mins. Stir in parsley.

Accompaniment
Peas

Table Setting
Try to emulate a Hungarian setting, checkered tablecloths, wooden forks and knives, oversized platters

Beverage
Hungarian red wine

Music
Issac Stern

Shrimp Fra Diavolo

Sensuousness

This is a recipe that I tried to imitate from one of the most romantic restaurants in New York City, a restaurant called Giordano's. Giordano's is in one of the seediest neighborhoods in New York, right at the foot of the Lincoln Tunnel on the New York side of 39th Street. Once inside it's a different world, it's dark but not pitch black, it's got flowers, an outdoor garden, and Mr. Giordano who I remember very fondly singing romantic songs of Trieste. This is a restaurant that I went to years ago when I worked in the garment industry and have gone back to many times since. Every time I eat Shrimp Fra Diavolo I think of the romance of Mr. Giordano.

Ingredients

1 lb shrimp, cleaned and deveined	3 Tbls chopped flat parsley
1 med onion, finely chopped	1 tsp sugar
3 cloves garlic, minced	1 tsp salt
4 Tbls olive oil	1 tsp oregano
1 - 1 lb can crushed Italian plum tomatoes	1 tsp dried basil
1 - 15 oz can tomato sauce	1 tsp cayenne pepper

Preparation

Cook and stir garlic and onions in hot oil in heavy Dutch oven until onion is tender. Stir in all ingredients except shrimp and simmer uncovered for 1 1/2 hours. Stir in shrimp and simmer an additional 5 mins.

Accompaniment   Linguini

Table Setting   Checkered Italian tablecloths, big wine goblets, pictures of Trieste, where Mr. Giordano came from

Beverage   Very robust, hearty Burgundy

Music   Sergio Franchi

Broiled Lamb with Currant Peaches

Sensuousness

When summer comes there is nothing better than the first rush of peaches - the smell and the feel of fresh peaches. There are few things that can describe the summer feeling you get from this fruit. This is my own recipe, mixing a meat with fruit, which I did back in the '60's, which today is a foundation of nouvelle cuisine.

Ingredients

6 rib lamb chops

3 peaches, pitted, cut in half, and very ripe

6 tsps currant jelly

2 tsps salt

1 tsp pepper

1 tsp garlic powder

Preparation

Preheat broiler to highest point. Sprinkle chops with salt, pepper, and garlic. Fill the peach halves with currant jelly. Place chops in broiler and broil 4 mins. on each side. Place peach halves in broiler. Broil another 3 mins.

Accompaniment

To really give a '60's flair have mint and red currant jelly on the side, mashed potatoes with strips of peaches on top, and buttered carrots

Table Setting

This is a dish I like to eat outdoors on a hard wood table or on a blanket spread out on a meadow on a very bright, sunny day

Beverage

A very cold and lusty Rosé wine

Music

Polka music

Chef's Salad Bowl

Sensuousness

After a while it has to happen - with all the cooking I do, weight has come upon me. This is a dish I look back on and still make as a diet dish although sometimes I do question it's "dietthicity"; however, it is one I serve on summer days to my wife who is also constantly on a diet now, thus, it brings me back to my memories of my first diet.

Ingredients

1/2 head Boston lettuce, cut into leaves

1/4 lb fresh turkey breasts in julienne strips

1/4 lb ham in julienne strips

1/4 lb Swiss cheese in julienne strips

1/2 cucumber, peeled and cut into wedges

6 radishes in wedges

1/2 cup olive oil

1 large fresh tomato in wedges

1 clove garlic, crushed

2 tsps salt

2 tsps freshly ground pepper

Juice of 1/2 lemon

Preparation

In a wooden salad bowl take crushed garlic and rub around bowl. Wash all vegetables carefully and refrigerate. Lay lettuce on bottom of bowl. Line with cucumbers, radishes, tomatoes. Put salt and pepper on them. Place meats and cheese in center. Mix olive oil and lemon juice. Pour dressing in center and toss well.

Accompaniment
Macaroni salad

Table Setting
To be eaten in the kitchen with candlesticks and good wooden plates

Beverage
Club soda

Music
Aerobic music

Shrimp Chef's Salad

Sensuousness

I look at dieting, which has never been one of my favorite things, in order to feel sensuous about myself. I like dieting on good food, and shrimp is one of my favorites. The below recipe is something I created years ago to fight the fat.

Ingredients

For salad

1 lb shrimp, cleaned and deveined

2 Tbls finely chopped dill

1 head Boston lettuce, shredded

3 Tbls capers

1 large tomato, quartered

Pinch curry powder

lemon dressing

For lemon dressing

3 Tbls lemon juice

1/2 tsp salt

1/8 tsp black pepper

1/4 tsp sugar

1/8 tsp Coleman mustard

1/2 cup olive oil

Preparation

For lemon dressing: Combine all ingredients except oil. Mix well in a bowl. Then pour oil in very slowly.

For salad: Boil water. Add shrimp. When water returns to boil, remove shrimp. Sprinkle with salt and dill. Chill. Tear lettuce leaves, wash well, and chill. Place shrimp on top of lettuce. Add tomatoes and capers. Mix well. Add dressing and curry powder. Toss lightly.

Accompaniment
Melba Toast

Table Setting
Nice to eat outdoors on a blanket

Beverage
Diet Coke

Music
Jane Fonda's Workout

Zucchini Sauce

Sensuousness

Zucchini Sauce was made in the summer of 1975. This was the first house that I had ever owned and the first home I had ever lived in. It was the second year of my marriage to lovely Sonia. I created this sauce from a little garden that we had grown in the backyard of our home in Ridgewood, New Jersey. Each day I watched the garden grow and one of the vegetables in the ground was zucchini. Such a beautiful flower comes and out of the flower emerges the zucchini squash. Very interesting, lifelike, very sensual.

Ingredients

1/4 cup olive oil

1 med onion, chopped

4 med zucchini, sliced

5 med tomatoes, peeled, seeded, and diced

1 clove garlic, minced

1 tsp salt

1 bay leaf

1 tsp ground pepper

3 Tbls chopped fresh basil

1/2 tsp oregano

Preparation

Heat oil in heavy Dutch oven. Saute onion and garlic until tender. Add zucchini, tomatoes, salt, bay leaf, pepper, basil, and oregano. Simmer, covered, for 15 mins. Uncover sauce and continue to simmer for 25 mins.

Accompaniment
Pasta and freshly grated cheese

Table Setting
Garden like, flowery tablecloths, flowery dishes and servingware, and a platter of vegetables in the center of the table

Beverage
May wine

Music
Songs from The Byrds

Scallopine à la Romano

Sensuousness

I have yet to find a veal dish that is tasty, romantic, and can be shared. This dish I had prepared about 10 years ago, where it came from I do not know and I shared this with a wonderful person who I have since not seen and I'd like to share this with you.

Ingredients

1 lb veal scallopine

1/4 lb butter

1/2 lb mushrooms, sliced

1 clove garlic, finely chopped

1 cup sherry

1/2 cup beef stock

1 tsp dried parsley

Preparation

Pound pieced of veal real thin. Saute in medium frying pan on medium heat in hot butter. Add mushrooms and garlic. Add sherry and beef stock. Simmer 3 mins. Add parsley and serve.

Accompaniment
A light pasta dish with butter and garlic

Table Setting
A white tablecloth, candelabra, long candlesticks

Beverage
Dry white Chablis

Music
Julius La Rosa

Caesar's Salad

Sensuousness

This dish really is made to impress your loved one. Set up a little stand by a table, get a large bowl, and mix the Caesar's Salad with great flourish and dramatics for your companion. This is a great dish, and one of my sister's favorites.

Ingredients

1 clove garlic, crushed

3/4 cup olive oil

1 head romaine

1 head chickory

1 tsp Worcestershire sauce

1 tsp salt

1 tsp freshly ground black pepper

1 egg, boil for 30 seconds

Juice of 1 lemon

3 oz Roquefort cheese

1/2 cup Parmesan cheese

2 cups homemade croutons

Preparation

Add garlic to the oil and let stand 1 hour. Tear greens apart with your hands and wash under ice cold water. Spin dry. Toss the greens with the oil and seasonings in a large bowl. Crack the egg into the greens and sprinkle with the lemon juice. Toss until greens are covered. Add cheese and toss again. Top with croutons and toss again.

Accompaniment   Rare filet mignon

Beverage   Bloody Caesars

Music   Frank Sinatra's 1940's music

Haussa Rice

Sensuousness

Haussa Rice is a Cuban dish. This always reminds me of my trips to Union City to see various friends and associates. Union City in New Jersey is a vibrant, lovely, full of life, sensuous Cuban town that is almost like a country unto itself.

Ingredients

1 lb carne seca dried beef*

3 1/2 cups raw rice

1/2 cup vegetable oil

2 cloves garlic, finely chopped

2 Tbls salt

7 cups very hot water

1/4 cup dried shredded unsweetened coconut

2 Tbls butter

3 med onions, thinly sliced

*Carne seca dried beef is available in Cuban or Spanish markets

Preparation

Put carne seca in mixing bowl. Cover with cold water and let stand overnight in a refrigerator, changing water occasionally. Drain and carefully scrape off the thick coating from the beef. Place beef in a saucepan. Add cold water to cover. Boil and drain. Repeat process twice. Let beef cool and cube it. Rinse the rice in several changes of cold water. Drain well. Heat oil in a deep saucepan. When very hot, add garlic and brown. Then add the rice. Stir 2 mins. and add salt. Cook 5 more minutes. Add water and coconut. Cover and cook 20 mins. Melt butter in a saucepan. Add the onions. Cook until wilted. Add the beef and cook until meat is very hot. Surround the rice with the meat and onion mixture.

Accompaniment
Onion and Avocado Salad

Table Setting
As Cuban as possible, even put pictures of Fidel Castro up, and I like a 1958 Chevrolet as a centerpiece and pass out cigars for this dish

Beverage
Rum punch

Music
Guantanamera sung by Pete Seeger

Roast Goose with Sage and Onion Stuffing

Sensuousness

Christmas, Easter, Passover, whatever, there was always the traditional turkey. Part of "Sensuous Cooking" is to instill, gradually, differences in food and tastes. Goose is a rich food, fatty like duck, bigger than the duck, more meat, and really deep, hearty flavor.

Ingredients

For goose

1 - 10 lb goose	1 cup water	1 clove garlic, sliced
2 cups dry white wine	1 med chopped onion	

For gravy

2 Tbls goose fat	6 Tbls flour	3 tsps salt
3 cups goose broth made from boiling the neck and the gizzards		

For stuffing

3 med onions, chopped	3/4 lb chopped mushrooms	1 tsp sage
1/2 lb butter	1/4 cup chopped parsley	1 pkg herb stuffing mix

Preparation

For stuffing: Saute the onions in 1/4 lb butter until transparent. Add the mushrooms, parsley, and sage. Saute, stirring 3 mins. Add this mixture to the herb stuffing.

For goose: Fill the cavity of the goose with the stuffing mix. Prick the entire surface of the goose with a sharp tined fork. Place goose in roasting pan. Pour the wine and water into the pan and add the onion and garlic. Roast about 3 1/4 hours. Remove goose and let rest about 15 mins.

For gravy: Skin the fat from the pan drippings, reserving 2 Tbls of fat. Add enough goose broth to make 3 cups of liquid. Return goose fat to roasting pan. While off the heat, add the flour and blend until smooth. Stir in the goose broth liquid and cook, stirring, over medium heat until it boils and it is thickened.

Accompaniment

Serve a lot of accompaniments with this - red cabbage boiled with vinegar and brown sugar, roasted potatoes, Brussels sprouts, candied yams, rutabaga

Table Setting

Very festive, a ceramic goose centerpiece, your best utensils and flatware

Beverage

Pilsner Beer

Music

Christmas carols

Veal Chops with Belgian Endive

Sensuousness

Belgian endive is a sexy vegetable, just take a look at it and your imagination can go wild.

Ingredients

4 large veal chops	2 Tbls water
2 tsps salt	3 shallots, finely chopped
1/4 cup flour	3 Tbls cognac
4 Tbls butter	1 1/2 cups heavy cream
4 firm white Belgian endives	1/4 cup Parmesan cheese

Preparation

Sprinkle chops on both sides with salt. Dredge in flour. Heat 3 Tbls butter in a heavy skillet. Place chops in one layer. Cook over moderate heat for 10 mins. Turn. Cook 15 mins. longer. Meanwhile, while chops are cooking, place endives in a heavy saucepan. Add 1 Tbls of butter, salt, and the water. Cover closely and simmer 20 mins. Be careful, not letting them burn. When chops are done, transfer chops to a warm platter and cover with foil. Add the shallots to the skillet and cook, stirring, with a wooden spoon for 30 secs. Add the cognac and flame it. Stirring to get the particles that cling to the bottom. Add the cream and cook over high heat, stirring. Strain the sauce into a saucepan. Put the chops into a baking dish. Press the endive gently to remove excess water. Arrange them around the chops. Spoon the sauce over all. Sprinkle with Parmesan and bake 15 mins.

Accompaniment
Pasta with garlic and oil

Table Setting
Toy soldiers on the table

Beverage
Fresca

Music
Shirley Bassey's Never, Never, Never

46

Oysters Chauveron

Sensuousness

In keeping with oyster dishes I don't have to say anything more. Let your imagination go wild and anything that works, let it work.

Ingredients

24 oysters on the half shell

1/2 cup finely chopped parsley

3 finely chopped shallots

1/2 lb butter at room temperature

3 Tbls plain bread crumbs

3 cloves garlic, finely chopped

Preparation

Open the oysters and leave on the half shell. Combine the chopped parsley and garlic in a mixing bowl. Add the remaining ingredients and blend well. Spoon this mixture on top of the oysters and bake 10 mins. in a 350º oven.

Table Setting

Nautical, a fish statue or fish plates

Beverage

Bullshots

Music

Theme from The French Foreign Legion

Roast Loin of Pork with Mustard

Sensuousness

This is a Sunday afternoon dish. If you are married, this is a good dish to bring the in-laws over to have. If you are not married, and have a squeeze, this is a good dish to bring your squeeze's relatives over for. Or if you're home alone on Sunday and watching football or baseball or basketball, it's a nice dish to have by yourself. It brightens up the senses and soothes the brain.

Ingredients

1 - 6 lb loin of pork with bone in

2 tsps salt

1/4 lb caul fat (also called net fat)

1/2 cup Dijon mustard

2 tsps dried thyme

1/2 lb onions

24 very small white onions

1 cup water

Preparation

Trim away some, but not all, of the fat of the pork. Sprinkle with salt. On a flat surface, open up the caul fat and place the pork, bone side down into it. Smear the mustard all over the pork. Sprinkle the thyme on various points of the pork. Bring up the edges of the caul fat to cover completely. Place the pork, bone side down, in a roasting pan. Bake, uncovered, at 350º for 30 mins. Thinly slice the onions and scatter around the pork. Scatter the small onions around the pork. Reduce the heat to 325º and bake 45 mins. Cover loosely with foil and bake 15 additional minutes. Remove the foil and cover the pork with a heavy lid and bake 30 mins. longer. Remove the pork, leaving the juices in the pan. Transfer pork to a serving dish and arrange small onions around it. Then make a pan gravy by adding the water to the pan juices.

Accompaniment

Potatoes sauteed in butter and cream

Table Setting

Something silly and frivolous for your relatives, maybe a Venus de Milo statue in the middle of the table

Beverage

Serve root beer

Music

As offensive as it can be to your relatives - rock and roll if they're old and classical if they're young; make this a frivolous day

Spanish Liver Pâté

Sensuousness

The two people who have made my life sensual, better, and a more compassionate one which I like to think of myself as, is my wife, who I've been married to for 20 lovely years, and a person who also means a lot to me, perhaps not in a sensuous way, but in a way that has been very predominant in my feelings, my sister, and every time I make this dish, Spanish Liver Pâté, I think of her, probably in the negative sense because she hates liver pâté and I never made it for her.

Ingredients

1 lb ground lean pork

1/2 lb ground chicken livers

1/2 lb ground beef liver

1 small onion, chopped

2 Tbls parsley

1 tsp ground pepper

1/2 tsp ground ginger

1/4 tsp cinnamon

3 tsps salt

3 Tbls brandy

8 strips bacon

Preparation

Grind and blend all the meats together. Add all the other ingredients and mix very thoroughly. Line a loaf pan with the strips of bacon. Pack the mixture in and bake 1 1/2 hours in a 350° oven. Cool the pâté under a lot of pressure, using cans with a plate under them to weigh it down. Drain all fat from the pâté and serve cold.

Accompaniment

French cornichons and black bread with butter

Table Setting

This could be used on a buffet table

Beverage

Sherry

Music

Julio Iglesias

Gazpacho Andaluz

Sensuousness

Every time I have Gazpacho I think of summertime. I also make a Gazpacho drink which is the soup which you can add a shot of vodka to. Very appealing, subtle, and tasteful.

Ingredients

6 large ripe tomatoes

1 large onion

3 cloves garlic

1 med cucumber, peeled

1/4 cup wine vinegar

1/2 cup olive oil

2 Tbls salt

4 cups water

Preparation

Chop all the vegetables coarsely and place in a processor and run at high speed. Strain well. Add the oil and vinegar. Mix it well. Refrigerate 1 hour. Add the water, mixing, and refrigerate until very cold.

Accompaniment

Chopped onions, chopped tomatoes, chopped cucumbers, and a little sour cream

Table Setting

Spanish, with perhaps pictures or prints of Picasso on the walls

Beverage

White Sangria

Music

Duke Ellington

Vitello Tonnato

Sensuousness

Probably one of the most romantic Italian dishes ever to be served. It is an appetizer that is beautiful. It is not inexpensive. This is sensual and sexy. The tuna sauce compliments the thin veal and it blasts your senses, very sultry.

Ingredients

1 1/2 lb veal cutlets

4 Tbls butter

4 Tbls olive oil

1 bunch parsley, chopped

1 large onion, chopped

8 cloves garlic

1 - 7 oz can tuna fish in olive oil

1/2 cup olive oil

1/4 cup butter, melted

1/4 cup dry white wine

2 Tbls lemon juice

1 tsp salt

1 tsp grated lemon rind

Preparation

Saute veal cutlets in butter and 4 Tbls of olive oil. Drain and refrigerate. In a blender combine all the other ingredients and whirl at high speed until smooth. Refrigerate. When cool, spoon the tuna sauce over the cold veal.

Accompaniment
A side dish of capers or even some red caviar

Table Setting
Your most elegant lace with fine champagne flutes and silverware

Beverage
Champagne

Music
Gladys Knight and the Pips

Scalloped Potatoes

Sensuousness

It fascinated me one day when I had dinner at a person's house that I was dating and she whipped out a box of Betty Crocker's Scalloped Potatoes. Her name was Janette, and to this day I can't quite forget that scene of being served potatoes out of a box. This is my own recipe that I have served throughout the years to various guests.

Ingredients

6 large potatoes, peeled and thinly sliced

4 Tbls all purpose flour

1/4 lb butter

1 large onion, diced

1 tsp paprika

1 tsp dry mustard

2 tsps salt

1 cup heavy cream

Preparation

In a circular baking dish, arrange the potatoes. Dot with butter. Sprinkle the onions on them, the salt, the dry mustard, and the flour. Keep repeating this step until you fill the pan to the top. When the top is filled, pour the cream over the potatoes. Sprinkle with paprika and bake in a 350° for 40 mins.

Accompaniment
This is a side dish that should be served with meats, especially steak

Table Setting
Lazy Susan centerpiece

Beverage
Russian Peppar Vodka

Music
Elton John

Shrimp and Scallop Mayonnaise

Sensuousness

An ideal summer dish. A dish that conjures up memories of being in Bangor, Maine. It is a dish to have on a hot summer day and is refreshing to the palate.

Ingredients

3/4 cup dry white wine

10 peppercorns

3 sprigs parsley

1/2 bay leaf

For mayonnaise

1 egg yolk

1 tsp wine vinegar

3 tsps Dijon mustard

1 shallot, sliced

1 clove garlic, sliced

1 1/2 lbs sea scallops, quartered

1 1/2 lbs shrimp, shelled and deveined

3 drops Tabasco

Juice of 1/2 lemon

1 cup olive oil

Preparation

Combine wine, peppercorns, parsley, thyme, bay leaf, shallots, garlic, and salt in a saucepan. Simmer 5 mins. Add the scallops. Cover and simmer 3 mins. Let cool. Scoop out the scallops and chill. Bring the cooking liquid to a boil and add the shrimp and simmer 3 mins. Let chill.

For mayonnaise: Place the egg yolk in a mixing bowl and add the vinegar, mustard, Tabasco, and salt. Beat vigorously for a minute or two with an electric beater. Being very slow, about a tablespoon at a time, add the oil and continue beating until fluffy. Combine the mayonnaise with the shrimps and scallops.

Accompaniment
Watercress Salad

Table Setting
Picnic blanket with red paper plates

Beverage
Maine Blueberry wine

Music
Country and Western

Chicken Saute with Watercress

Sensuousness

This is one of the best dishes I have ever made in my 27 years of cooking. I have made this repeatedly from small dinner parties, which this is a recipe for, to very large gatherings. It is a dish that is easy to prepare and so delicious.

Ingredients

2 bunches crisp watercress

3 Tbls salt

1 - 3 lb broiler/fryer chicken, cut into serving pieces

3 Tbls butter

2 shallots, finely chopped

1/2 cup dry white wine

1 cup heavy cream

Preparation

Trim watercress stems. Drop watercress into boiling, salted water. Note: use a lot of salt, it keeps the watercress green. Cook after water returns to the boil about 3 mins. Drain and run under cold water to chill. Pat to dry. Put watercress in blender but do not overblend. Salt chicken. Heat 2 Tbls butter in a heavy skillet. Cook chicken, skin side down, about 5 mins. Reduce heat. Turn chicken and cook 20 mins. on other side. Turn pieces as necessary. Transfer chicken to a warm platter. Pour off most of the fat but leave 1 Tbl. Add the shallots and cook about 1 min. Add the wine and cook over high heat until wine is reduced by half, stirring with a wooden spoon to dissolve brown particles that cling to the pan. Add the heavy cream and cook over high heat, stirring, about 5 mins. Add the watercress and stir. Return chicken to sauce with any juices that have accumulated. Swirl in a pat of butter and serve.

Accompaniment
Wild and domestic rice mixture

Table Setting
I like a farm setting with this with maybe a little animal as a centerpiece

Beverage
Elderberry wine

Music
Kenny Rogers' country and western music

Shrimp with Anchovy Tomato Sauce

Sensuousness

Many people when they think of the lowly anchovy get all excited; I hate anchovies, I dislike anchovies, I can't stand anchovies! Well I personally do not like anchovy pizza but I do love anchovies. A Caesar's Salad without anchovies is not a Caesar's Salad and then again life without anchovies, what would that be, a life without anchovies? I guess it's not as bad as having a fatal disease, but, the anchovy is such a lowly creature, that adds so much to a dish, even if it makes you thirsty; isn't it fun drinking together?

Ingredients

3 lbs shrimp, cleaned and deveined

8 Tbls olive oil

4 tsps finely minced garlic

2 - 28 oz cans plum tomatoes

2 tsps oregano

2 Tbls fresh minced basil

5 Tbls anchovy paste

3/4 lb mushrooms, thinly sliced

2 dried hot red peppers, crushed

1/2 cup drained capers

Preparation

Heat 1/2 the olive oil in a small skillet with 1/2 the garlic. Cook briefly and add the tomatoes, oregano, 1/2 of the basil, salt, and pepper. Cook, stirring often, about 30 mins. Add the anchovy paste. Heat the remaining oil in another pan. Add the shrimp, the remaining garlic, and basil, and mushrooms. Cook, stirring, until shrimp are red, about 2 mins. Add the shrimp mixture to the sauce. Add the hot pepper, capers, salt, and pepper. Bring just to the boil and serve.

Accompaniment

This makes a great sauce to be served over linguini

Table Setting

I like a nautical Portuguese type table setting with rustic candlesticks and nautical setting, wear a striped shirt for dining in this with white pants

Beverage

Portuguese red wine

Music

Theme from Underwater, which was a 1954 movie with Gilbert Roland and Terry Moore

Italian Hen

Sensuousness

This is a copy of a dish that I had when I was only 16 years old. It brings back fond memories of a land that, even growing up in Brooklyn, was foreign to me, this land being Bensonhurst. Bensonhurst in Brooklyn is an Italian section with Italian cheese stores and pork stores and it even has an oil store. It was a new world to me coming from Park Slope and the Irish section of Brooklyn these feelings that I feel today heighten my sensuality and my sensitiveness towards other people.

Ingredients

2 whole Cornish game hens, split

3 Tbls melted butter

1/2 lb finely chopped spinach

1/2 lb finely diced fresh mozzarella

3 slices thick prosciutto, diced

1/2 cup garlic croutons

1 tsp thyme

1 tsp sage

Preparation

Boil spinach 1 min. in unsalted water. Drain well. Pat dry. Combine with the rest of the ingredients to make the stuffing. Stuff the hens with the stuffing of spinach, mozzarella, and prosciutto, and garlic croutons. Brush with melted butter. Salt them and bake 1 hour and 10 mins.

Accompaniment

Salad of arugola, dandelions, and romaine lettuce with an oil dressing and small potatoes sauteed in butter and parsley

Table Setting

A jovial setting, bright dish ware, bright tablecloth, big candelabra

Beverage

Dandelion wine

Music

Music from Moonglow

Fish Saute Romagnole

Sensuousness

When I was old enough to date, about 16, and I first really became interested in food, I took out a girl named Diana. She came from a very large Italian family and I had dinner there almost every Sunday night - I think much to her father's chagrin. I believe they hated me because I was not Italian and also very young. This is one of the dishes that they made and which I have tried to copy for my book. Sensuousness is really fun when you're 16, it's better when you're almost 50.

Ingredients

2 cloves garlic, finely minced

1 Tbls finely chopped parsley

4 Tbls olive oil

2 lb haddock fillet, cut into small pieces

1 1/2 cups Italian plum tomatoes, drained

1/4 cup dry white wine

2 tsps salt

1 tsp dried thyme

Preparation

In a heavy casserole, saute gently the garlic and parsley in olive oil. Add the fish, Saute over low flame for 5 mins. Caution: do not let fish stick. Add the tomatoes, wine, salt, and thyme. Cover tightly and simmer for 20 mins.

Accompaniment

Pasta with garlic and oil and an arugola salad

Table Setting

White tablecloth and posters of Bensonhurst. Add a centerpiece consisting of fruits.

Beverage

Italian Chianti wine

Music

Music from Barber of Seville

Angels in Blankets

Sensuousness

This is an old recipe used in the '50's at cocktail parties, and when giving a party it makes for a festive, interesting appetizer and easy to make. The beauty of it, is the name, Angels. Shrimp are like a delicate, fluffy white cloud of angels.

Ingredients

1 1/4 lb large shrimps

1/2 lb bacon

1/3 cup prepared mustard, preferably Dijon

30 toothpicks

Preparation

Wash and dry the shrimps thoroughly and devein them. Cut bacon in half and spread bacon with mustard. Wrap shrimp in the bacon/mustard combination and secure with a toothpick. Preheat broiler for 5 mins. and broil shrimp for 4 mins. on one side. Turn and broil another 1 min.

Accompaniment
Champagne

Table Setting
This should be a pass around hors d'oeuvre

Beverage
Champagne

Music
Romantic hits of The Beatles

Braised Breast of Lamb with Beans

Sensuousness

Oh, is breast of lamb such an abused piece of meat! A lot of people find breast of lamb not to be romantic because it is fatty. When cooked right, this recipe should not only not be fatty but the beans that are added with it make for such a luxurious and hearty dinner, almost fat free. This is to be served on a snowy wintry day.

Ingredients

4 lbs breast of lamb, cut into serving pieces

3 Tbls salt

2 Tbls black pepper

1 Tbls rosemary

1 Tbls garlic powder

1 med onion, sliced

1 1/2 cups water

8 oz cut green beans

1/2 lb baby lima beans

Preparation

Brown lamb pieces very slowly in heavy Dutch oven. Pour off all the fat. Sprinkle the meat with the salt, pepper, and rosemary. Add onion and cook very slowly, covered, adding a little water at a time for about 2 hours and 20 mins. 15 mins. before serving stir in the vegetables with some more water.

Accompaniment
Boiled parsley potatoes

Table Setting
Basket of dried flowers on the table

Beverage
A warm drink, warm red wine or even warm brandy

Music
Theme from show music, Oklahoma

Baked Spiced Chicken

Sensuousness

Here is a Sunday afternoon chicken dish. This brings back memories of home, and is to be served on a warm Sunday afternoon or a cold Sunday afternoon, where you can add ingredients proportionately to make it into a family feast.

Ingredients

1 broiler/fryer chicken, cut into 8 pieces

3 Tbls butter

Juice of 1/2 lemon

2 cloves, minced

2 Tbls paprika

1 Tbls allspice

1 Tbls ground pepper

2 Tbls salt

1 tsp poultry seasoning

1 tsp cumin

1 cup dry white wine

Preparation

Pat chicken dry. Sprinkle all the spices on both sides of the chicken, kneading the spices into the chicken. Place on a large baking pan. Sprinkle with the lemon juice. Put slices of lemon on sides of pan. Pour wine over top. Top with the butter and bake at 400º for 1 hour.

Accompaniment
Baked potatoes with sour cream and chives

Table Setting
Sunday best with wine glasses and assorted serving pieces that make it a Sunday feast

Beverage
A Sunday iced tea or a Mint Julep

Music
Music from Shirley Bassey

60

Basic Frittata

Sensuousness

A lazy Sunday, Springtime, what to do to please your lover? Make an elegant breakfast and a frittata is one of the best. It is more than just an omelet, it is a frittata and is meant to be served in bed on a bed board.

Ingredients

4 eggs

2 tsps heavy cream

1/2 tsp salt

5 Tbls grated Parmesan cheese

1 cup finely chopped fresh spinach

3 Tbls chopped parsley

1 med onion, finely chopped

1 clove garlic, minced

1 Tbls olive oil

Preparation

Beat eggs lightly. Mix in remaining ingredients except oil. Heat oil in an omelet pan. Pour in egg mixture. Cook over low heat. When eggs begin to set, give a flip to form an omelet or leave whole and just empty onto a plate.

Table Setting

Breakfast in bed with a red rose on the bed board

Beverage

Mimosa and dark, rich, strong coffee

Music

The Association album

Insalata Di Vova

Sensuousness

When I see people eating at work I say, "Can't a lunch be a little bit better? Can't it be better than a McDonald's hamburger or a Burger King?" This is a very, very simple egg salad that can be brought to work and shared with your fellow workers.

Ingredients

4 hard boiled eggs, sliced

3 Tbls olive oil

1 Tbls white wine vinegar

1 1/2 tsps salt

1 Tbls freshly ground pepper

2 scallions, chopped

1 stalk celery, diced

1 tsp parsley

Preparation

Arrange eggs on a platter over a bed of lettuce. Combine all the other ingredients in a bottle. Shake well and pour over the egg salad.

Accompaniment
Black cup of coffee and toast

Table Setting
At your office, on a blotter

Beverage
Coffee, tea, or milk

Music
Whatever Muzak is being pumped in to your office

An Appealing Human Story of Those Who Follow a Scarlet Thread in the Search for the Sweets of Life!

Sophisticated humor, deep human feeling, touches of pathos, inspired dialogue—in a drama of husbands who give their own wives everything but love—and wives who refuse to pay for marriage by boredom! *A Real Treat for the Box-Office—and the Patrons of Your Theatre!*

Chapter Three

Out of Town Sensuousness

Travelling is romance unto itself. When you go to different places and see different sites your awareness and senses are heightened. A trip, wherever it may be, brings a feeling of relaxation to the body. Stresses of everyday evaporate and you appreciate things in a different light. Never travel with the idea "If it's Tuesday, it must be Belgium." Explore on your own. Don't eat American food in foreign countries. Try and learn the language of the country you are in. Notice the people. See how they conduct themselves. Be proud to be an American, but in Italy, try to eat like an Italian.

In "Sensuous Cooking" you don't have to travel far to heighten your senses. If you live in a rural area of a state go to a major city. If you live in a city go camping. Always be prepared to prepare yourself for the unexpected.

When my wife and I went to Yugoslavia in 1986 it was considered adventurous; but, actually we made our own adventure. We made the trip exotic.

I have been fortunate to do extensive travelling and even with certain handicaps and lack of amenities, my travels have always been wonderful. Each time I come home from a trip I feel I absorbed more of the land, sea and world around me.

Brooklyn Pot Roast

Sensuousness

The sense that Brooklyn Pot Roast appeals to is the sense of a home, of old times, family, and being young; this is not a recipe of today's cooking styles. This is a recipe that is to transport the maker back to the time of his/her youth, a time when we had no responsibilities, when we woke up and the biggest decision we had to make was whether to go to school or not, in the summer whether to go to the pool or not, or to work or not. These are also the images that this recipe will bring to mind, the images of being back home. For me, Brooklyn Pot Roast is back to my home in Brooklyn, my mother who cooked pot roast like every other mother did, and a family who sat down to dinner, usually on Sunday, to have pot roast. And what makes this particular pot roast Sensuous is that it is being made for a new generation of loved ones. It is a recipe that is too easily forgotten, mishandled, and mistreated. Sensuous Cooking hopes to heighten the images and senses of pot roast.

Ingredients

4 lbs boneless chuck or rump or round

4 Tbls of seasoned flour*

3 Tbls canola oil

2 Tbls prepared mustard

2 large onions, sliced

1 bay leaf

3 cups water

1 tsp salt

1 tsp pepper

*Seasoned flour is flour mixed with 1 tsp salt and 1 tsp freshly ground pepper

Preparation

Rub the chuck or rump or round with seasoned flour. In a Dutch oven, brown meat on all sides over medium heat. Spread top of meat with mustard and add rest of ingredients. Bring to boil and simmer for 2 1/2 hours.

For the gravy, skim fat from pot juices, done easily by adding ice cubes to the pot and quickly removing the cubes; the fat will have congealed on the cubes. Mix 1 Tbls flour to 1 Tbls cold water for each cup of pan juices. Gradually stir in the flour/water combination and cook over low heat to boiling. Boil 1 min., add salt and pepper, and place in gravy boat.

Accompaniment   Mashed potatoes, peas and carrots

Table Setting   Should be shared with parents, if still alive, or loved ones, aunts and uncles. Serve on your best Sunday china with silver forks and knives.

Beverage   Brooklyn Beer

Music   Florian Zabach

Salad Niçoise

Sensuousness

I first had this dish in one of the five most romantic cities in the world. I had Salad Niçoise on the waterfront of Marseille and I suggest serving Salad Niçoise by a picturesque waterfront. If you don't have an ocean, a lake, a river, a stream, a pond, or a swimming pool by you, then take Salad Niçoise to the bathtub. Salad Niçoise just goes so wonderful with a water environment.

Ingredients

2 med ripe tomatoes, quartered

1 head romaine lettuce

3/4 cup extra virgin olive oil

1/4 cup white wine vinegar

2 cans - 7 oz tuna fish packed in olive oil, well drained

3 hard boiled eggs - halved

1 can rolled anchovy fillets

12 Greek olives

1 tsp salt

1/4 lb Provolone cheese, cut into slices

1 tsp salt

2 tsps freshly ground black pepper

Preparation

Wash lettuce and tomatoes in ice cold water. Let chill. Combine the oil and vinegar to form the dressing. In a salad bowl, tear lettuce into pieces and toss with part of the dressing. On top of the lettuce bed, arrange the tomatoes, eggs, tuna, anchovies, and olives. Pour remaining dressing on it. Sprinkle freshly ground black pepper and toss lightly.

Accompaniment

Side order of potato dill salad

Table Setting

As nautical as possible, put fish nets around you, eat with a black and white polo shirt, white pants with drawstrings

Beverage

Dry white wine

Music

Liszt

65

Veal and Onion Stew

Sensuousness

This dish can be confused with a Veal Marengo. However, this recipe is not truly French in origin. It is a dish to be put on a Sunday brunch table and again the romanticism is up to you - French, brunch, whatever.

Ingredients

1 3/4 lb roasting veal fillet, cubed

3 Tbls flour

1 tsp salt

1 tsp white pepper

4 Tbls olive oil

10 med onions, sliced

1 cup water

4 carrots, scraped and sliced

Preparation

Combine flour, salt, pepper and dust the meat well. Brown meat in hot oil in heavy skillet over medium heat. Add onions. Saute over low heat for 15 mins. Add water and cover. Bring to the boil. Reduce heat and simmer 1 1/4 hours. Add carrots and simmer another 15 mins.

Accompaniment
Buttered noodles

Table Setting
Informal, this is a dish to be eaten in the kitchen. It is a hearty dish. A buffet table is good for this dish, or even a Sunday morning breakfast.

Beverage
A lot of onions produces a sweet sauce, I like a tawny port with it

Music
Theme from Carmen

Veal Marengo

Sensuousness

This is the famous French veal dish that Napoleon courted Desiree with and served to his troops when fighting the English. It is romantic and it is French.

Ingredients

2 lbs stewing veal, cubed

3 Tbls olive oil

4 ripe tomatoes, peeled, seeded, and chopped

1 dozen tiny whole onions

2 Tbls flour

1 cup dry white wine

2 cups chicken stock

1 clove garlic, minced

1 tsp salt

1 tsp white pepper

Preparation

Brown veal in heavy casserole in olive oil. Add tomatoes and onions. Simmer about 5 mins. Sprinkle on flour and blend in thoroughly. Add wine, consomme, garlic, salt, and pepper. Cover and simmer 1 hour. Add sauteed mushrooms and simmer 1/2 hour more.

Accompaniment
Buttered noodles along with carrots

Table Setting
As French and Napoleonic as possible, big, huge wooden candlesticks, big platters or wooden bowls

Beverage
Cinzano

Music
Vicki Carr singing French songs

Chicken Provencale

Sensuousness

This recipe transports me back to a place in time, this place - the Provence region of France where cooking takes such tremendous bounds in the pleasures and the offerings it has to the senses. Chicken Provencale was a dish I had in Nice, which I loved and I'd like to share this with you. This makes a very, very fine festive dish to be served with family and friends.

Ingredients

1 whole roasting chicken, about 6 lbs

1/2 lb ground pork

2 cups wilted chopped spinach

1 tsp dried sage

1 tsp thyme

3 Tbls chopped pistachio nuts

2 Tbls Kosher salt

1 egg, beaten

1 boiled egg, medium hard

2 cloves garlic, crushed

3 Tbls olive oil

Preparation

Wash chicken. Dry well. In a bowl, place the pork, spinach, sage, thyme, pistachio nuts, 1 tsp salt, beaten egg and mix well. Stuff the chicken, placing the hard cooked egg in the center of the stuffing. Preheat oven to 375°. Crush the garlic in the oil and rub the chicken well with this mixture. Place chicken on a rack in a roasting pan and roast for 1 hour and 15 mins.

Accompaniment
Boiled potatoes

Table Setting
As close to Provence as possible, bright sunny, airy type of fixtures, posters, seashells on the table

Beverage
Dry white Chablis

Music
Theme from A Man And A Woman

Stuffed Mussels

Sensuousness

Mussels are today, like they were 20 years ago, an inexpensive shellfish dish to make. Mussels are so prominent in Belgium that they even have a mussel festival and every time I think of mussel dishes, I think of Belgium, the Flemish people, the French people, the German people, and their love for the mussels.

Ingredients

4 dozen mussels*

1 cup dry white wine

2/3 cup water

3 med onions, minced

1/3 cup olive oil

2/3 cup raw rice

1/2 cup pignoli nuts

2/3 cup tomato sauce

1 tsp allspice

2/3 cup currants

1 clove garlic, minced

*Scrub mussels well soak in cold water and cayenne pepper for 45 mins. to remove sand

Preparation

Put mussels in Dutch oven. Add water and wine. Steam for 10 mins. or until shells open. Discard unopened shells. Strain, reserving broth, adding enough water to make 2 1/2 cups of broth. In another Dutch oven, saute onions in oil until golden. Add rice and nuts. Saute until golden, stirring constantly. Add reserved cooking liquid, tomato sauce, allspice, and currants. Cover and simmer 15 mins. Turn off heat and let stand 10 mins. Toss mussels that have been taken out of their shells into this mixture.

Accompaniment
Sauted mushrooms and a Greek Salad

Table Setting
Elegant, maybe put books of Hercule Poirot on the dining room table

Beverage
Iced Clamato

Music
Yves Montand

Leg of Lamb with Flageolets

Sensuousness

This is a simple roast, something to have on Easter rather than ham or turkey or for any holiday, it is a festive dish. It is one that brightens up the day. It is French in origin and the French have a great way with lamb. This is a recipe that I have called on from a trip to France which is the most romantic country on earth.

Ingredients

1 lb dried flageolets

1 lb onions, thinly sliced

4 Tbls olive oil

2 lbs potatoes, unpeeled and thinly sliced

2 Tbls salt

1 cup beef bouillon

2 bay leaves

1 - 7 lb leg of lamb

1 tsp rosemary

Preparation

Cover beans with cold water. Cover and refrigerate overnight. Drain beans and drop into 2 quarts of boiling water. Cover and simmer 45 mins. or until tender. Drain. Saute onions in hot oil until golden. In a baking dish, layer half of the potatoes, onions, and beans. Repeat layering. Add bouillon with bay leaves and heat to boiling. Pour over vegetables. Rub lamb with rosemary. Put on top of vegetables and bake, uncovered, for 3 hours.

Accompaniment

Flageolets are a French bean and I like a baked potato with sour cream and chives and yogurt with this dish

Table Setting

For a centerpiece, daffodil flowers, your best chinaware and glassware

Beverage

Cognac

Music

Montevani

Shrimp à la Moutarde des Meaux

Sensuousness

Everything in French sounds so much better than in English. Pronounce the word for mustard, in French, moutarde. Let the name roll off your tongue. Say it a few times and all of sudden, mustard becomes such a romantic ingredient.

Ingredients

2 lbs shrimp, shelled, deveined, and cut in half	6 shallots, finely chopped
5 Tbls butter	1/2 cup dry white wine
4 Tbls flour	1/4 cup finely chopped parsley
2 cups milk	1 egg yolk
1 Tbls salt	4 Tbls imported French Dijon mustard
1/4 tsp cayenne pepper	1/2 cup grated Parmesan cheese

Preparation

In a saucepan melt 3 Tbls butter and stir in the flour with a wire whisk. Stir in the milk, stirring rapidly. Season with salt and cayenne. Simmer 15 mins., stirring occasionally. In another saucepan combine the wine, shallots, and parsley. Cook over high heat until wine is almost totally reduced. Add this to the white sauce and cook 10 mins., stirring occasionally. Beat the egg yolk lightly and add to the sauce, stirring rapidly. Remove from heat and add 3 Tbls of mustard. Melt 2 Tbls of butter in a skillet and add the shrimp and cook until shrimp turn red. Add 1 Tbls of mustard and stir to coat. Add 1/3 of the sauce and stir to coat. Spoon the shrimp into ramekins or scallop shells. Spoon sauce over each. Top with Parmesan and bake in a 350° oven 10 - 15 mins.

Accompaniment
Endive and Radicchio Salad

Table Setting
A centerpiece of a big vase with winter flowers

Beverage
Dry white wine

Music
Edith Piaf

Florentine Beef Steak

Sensuousness

For years this has been one of my favorite beef recipes. It is delicious and gives off a bright light feeling. When I eat Florentine Beef Steak I think of the first time I had it in a restaurant call Ceceze in Florence, and it is so simple, but yet so delicious. I had this with a woman I had met on a plane going to Florence.

Ingredients

1 1/2 lb, 1 inch thick sirloin steak

4 Tbls extra virgin olive oil

2 Tbls freshly ground pepper

2 Tbls salt

Juice of 1/2 lemon

Preparation

Rub steak on both sides with olive oil and pepper. Let stand for 1 hour. Preheat broiler to highest setting for 20 mins. Broil steak 4 mins. on each side. Remove to platter. Salt it and squeeze the lemon juice on it.

Accompaniment

Risotto with anchovies and mashed turnips

Table Setting

It's hard to duplicate Florence, but if you can, murals, pictures, lots of candlesticks on the table, lots of light and cheerfulness

Beverage

Cinzano

Music

Pavarotti

Steak Tartare

Sensuousness

This is a recipe that I can never duplicate as well as I've had it in Yugoslavia. Everybody laughed when I went to Yugoslavia but it's such a romantic country. The way they do Steak Tartare is with such fanfare, sometimes 1/2 hour to 45 minutes at table side preparing it, each drop of spices just blended and folded in with love and affection. This is a dish that brings out the heroic love in people.

Ingredients

2 lbs leanest ground fillet mignon

2 tsps Dijon mustard

2 raw egg yolks

1 med onion, minced

The accouterments

2 hard boiled eggs

3 tsps red caviar, salmon

3 tsps black caviar, preferably Beluga

2 tsps salt

1 tsp cracked black peppercorns

1 tsp Worcestershire sauce

3 Tbls mayonnaise

Chopped parsley

capers

Preparation

Spread meat on waxed paper. Spread with mustard then egg yolks. Sprinkle with onion, salt, pepper, Worcestershire, and then blend kneading everything into the meat. Arrange in small patties on a platter and decorate with hard cooked eggs, with dollops of mayonnaise and dollops of caviar. Sprinkle with parsley and capers.

Accompaniment
Rye crisps, melba toast, fresh white toast

Table Setting
A nice dish to eat on picnics in the summer time on a blanket

Beverage
Slivowitz

Music
Yugoslavian music, Boris Kartoff is a real fun rock musician from Yugoslavia

Chicken Seville

Sensuousness

I first had Chicken Seville in Spain and it was shared with 3 other people from America who were visiting Spain as I was. They did not like the food, nor the hours that the Spanish people ate, mainly dinner about 10 or 11 o'clock. I had this dish that brings back the memories of this country, and I now wish to share it with you.

Ingredients

1 broiler/fryer, cut up	1 tsp salt
3 Tbls Spanish olive oil	1 tsp ground ginger
2 cloves garlic, minced	1 tsp paprika
10 oz chicken broth	1 1/2 tsps cornstarch
2 med oranges, peeled and sliced	1/2 cup pimento stuffed olives
1/2 cup thinly sliced celery	

Preparation

Brown chicken in hot oil in heavy casserole. Stir in garlic, chicken broth, orange, celery, salt, and ginger. Cook over low heat for 40 mins. Remove chicken. Blend cornstarch with 1 Tbls water. Stir into sauce. Stir in olives and cook over low heat until sauce boils for 2 mins. Pour sauce over chicken.

Accompaniment
Rice or noodles

Table Setting
As Spanish as you can make it - little castanets perhaps on the table, Spanish figurines

Beverage
Dry Sherry

Music
Music from Otello

Spanish Chicken Casserole

Sensuousness

This recipe, again, goes back to days when I was in Europe, and this particular dish was one I had in Spain. Europe is all so romantic, but, then again, romance is a state of mind. Coming back from Spain this dish brought memories to me.

Ingredients

1 broiler/fryer chicken, cut up into 8 parts

1 Tbls salt

1 tsp ground pepper

1/4 cup olive oil

18 oz tomato sauce with onions

8 oz tomato sauce with fresh mushrooms

2 cups water

1 cup uncooked rice

1/2 lb fresh peas, shelled

1/2 cup sliced ripe olives

Preparation

Sprinkle chicken with salt and pepper. Brown in heavy casserole in hot olive oil. Stir in the tomato sauces, salt, pepper, and rice. Stir in the water. Simmer, covered, 45 mins. Add peas and olives. Simmer 15 mins. more.

Table Setting

Bright, red plates, bright silverware, flute glasses

Beverage

Spanish white wine

Music

Spanish Flamenco

Steamed Blue Crabs

Sensuousness

Just a basic, simple preparation for a dish that is very messy and very easy to make. It is a dish that goes back to my childhood in the Sheepshead Bay section of Brooklyn. The romance of it is being messy together, cleaning crabs together, picking out meat, swapping crabs. Part of the fun of Steamed Blue Crabs is catching them. When I was young I caught these crabs at Jamaica Bay with my father. As I grew older I shared them with many people, I guess some people would say it is not romantic bathing in crab juice - you decide.

Ingredients

12 live blue crabs

3 cups water

Dash salt

Dash pepper

Sauces

Butter Sauce

1/4 cup melted sweet butter

Dash Worcestershire sauce

Dash Tabasco

Hot Sauce

4 Tbls ketchup

1 tsp Tabasco

1 tsp horseradish

Juice of 1/4 lemon

Preparation

In 3 cups boiling water, plunge the 12 crabs. Cover and steam for 15 mins. or until red. Set aside and cool. Then break the claws and crack them. Remove meat. Pull the button on the bottom of the belly of the crab and peel back the shell. Commence removing meat and serve with the sauces which are prepared by mixing the ingredients together.

Table Setting

Outside on a red picnic table with a plastic tablecloth and lots and lots of paper towels. Bibs should be used instead of napkins.

Beverage

Ballantine Ale

Creole Lamb Stew

Sensuousness

New Orleans is life, not to say any other city in the world is not life because you make your own life. A city even as remote or insignificant as any one you may think of can be life if you put it into it. New Orleans just adds that extra zest, the appreciation of fine food and drink and continuous hours. This is another recipe dedicated to that town.

Ingredients

2 lbs lamb neck, stew pieces

12 oz tomato sauce

1 tsp Worcestershire sauce

1/8 tsp garlic powder

1 tsp salt

1 tsp freshly ground pepper

1 tsp cayenne pepper

8 pearl onions

1 lb mushrooms, sliced

1 med green pepper, diced

2 Tbls water mixed with 1 Tbls flour

Preparation

Brown lamb in skillet without fat. Pour off the fat that comes from the meat. Add tomato juice, Worcestershire sauce, and spices. Cover and cook 45 mins. over low heat. Add onions, mushrooms, and pepper. Cover and cook 45 mins. more. Stir in the flour and water combination gradually to the sauce until thickened. Serve on a platter.

Accompaniment
Rice and french fried okra

Table Setting
Masks on the dining room wall go nice, even bustieres. Dress as sexy as possible, underwear, negligee; for men a tuxedo, a dark evening suit; and for a woman, maybe nothing. Or for a man, nothing, and a woman, an evening gown.

Beverage
Five Star Beer

Music
Louis Armstrong

Malibu Beach Mussels Maison

Sensuousness

The images that Malibu Beach Mussels Maison brings to my mind is a one day excursion I had to Malibu Beach. I saw so many things there - surfing, fishing, crabbing, clamming, building sand castles. It was like a salute to the sea. I created this dish for Malibu Beach.

Ingredients

3 lbs mussels	1 tsp white pepper
1/3 cup dry white wine	Juice of 1 lemon
1/3 cup wine vinegar	1/4 lb butter
1 Tbls dried oregano	Dash Worcestershire sauce
1 tsp salt	Dash Tabasco

Preparation

Place mussels in a large bowl. Cover with cold water. Add red pepper. This will clean the mussels without you having to scrub them to remove the sand. Remove the beards from said mussels. Put mussels in heavy kettle. Add wine, vinegar, salt, oregano, pepper, and lemon juice. Bring to the boil. Cover until mussels open. Cook 3 mins. Melt butter in separate pan. Add Worcestershire and Tabasco. Place mussels on a platter, preferably red or white. Put butter dunking sauce into a heat warming pot and dunk mussels into butter.

Accompaniment
Good french bread

Table Setting
As Californian as you can make it. Dress in printed shirts or shorts, bathing suits even. Have the table as casually set as possible.

Beverage
Evian water

Music
Beach Boys

Ratatouille à la Marseille

Sensuousness

This recipe is what I thought of after a trip to France. Whenever I make this dish I think of the harbor in Marseille, which is unlike any other harbor except for Hong Kong. The boats that are there, the people in their striped tee shirts, the berets, oh, just, oh, vive la France!

Ingredients

1 lb eggplant, peeled* and cubed

1/2 lb peeled zucchini, cubed

1/2 cup or more olive oil

1 large onion, sliced

2 green peppers, sliced

2 med tomatoes, cubed

3 cloves garlic, minced

2 tsps salt

1 tsp ground pepper

*I do not peel my eggplant nor do I put it in salt to drain the water

Preparation

Saute eggplant and zucchini in olive and remove with slotted spoon. Saute onion and green pepper until tender. Add tomatoes, garlic, eggplant, and zucchini. Sprinkle with salt and pepper. Cover and simmer until tender, about 1/2 hour.

Table Setting

Romantic. Pictures and posters of Paris, fancy wine goblets, fancy candlesticks, checkered tablecloth, or maybe go for your white tablecloth or green, bright lights.

Beverage

Kronenbourg Beer

Music

Bizet

Lobster Fra Diavolo à la Bay Ridge

Sensuousness

Lobster Fra Diavolo goes back to my days of Sheepshead Bay and Bay Ridge in Brooklyn. I guess one thing I will always remember about Lobster Fra Diavolo is its messiness. It is not an easy dish to eat, it is sloppy, but delicious. I hope that you think as much when you eat this dish about your own hometown as I do about mine.

Ingredients

1 - 2 lb live lobster

6 Tbls olive oil

1 tsp salt

1 tsp ground pepper

2 cloves garlic, finely chopped

1/4 cup finely chopped shallots

1 med green pepper, finely chopped

4 hot red peppers, chopped

4 cups Italian canned tomatoes

2 Tbls tomato paste

1/2 cup chopped flat parsley

1 tsp dried basil

1 tsp dried thyme

1 bay leaf

1 tsp dried oregano

12 little neck clams

Preparation

Kill lobster by putting it under warm running water until lobster passes away. Cut lobster into serving pieces by chopping up the tail, the claws, and the body. Remove liver and coral; set aside for the sauce. Heat lobster in kettle in oil. Add salt and pepper. Cook until bright red. When red, add the garlic and shallots. Add 1/2 cup red wine and cook till most of the wine evaporates. Add rest of ingredients except clams. Cover and simmer 15 mins. Add clams and liver. Cook until clams open.

Accompaniment
Serve Lobster Fra Diavolo over linguini

Table Setting
Very messy - no napkins, no pretty plates, lots of paper towels, nutcrackers and nut pickers, little cocktail forks, and perhaps, a hammer

Beverage
Rheingold beer

Music
Italian opera or Spanish Flamenco

Shrimp Creole New Orleans

Sensuousness

This New Orleans dish is lively and fiery. It brings good life, it enjoys. It is a recipe that conjures up memories of nights spent in New Orleans, the rustiness of the city, the anything goes attitude. This is a recipe to just let yourself go, enjoy, be natural, even eat naked.

Ingredients

1 1/2 cups chopped onion

1 cup chopped celery

2 med green peppers, chopped

2 cloves garlic, finely minced

1/4 cup butter

15 oz tomato sauce

1 cup water

1 tsp salt

1 tsp cayenne pepper

2 bay leaves, crushed

1 lb cleaned shrimp

Preparation

Cook and stir onion, celery, pepper, and garlic in melted butter for about 5 mins. Remove from heat. Stir in tomato sauce, water, and spices. Simmer 10 mins. Add shrimp. Heat to boiling, cover, and cook over medium heat for 10 mins.

Table Setting

Checkered tablecloth in blue and white, white plates, hearty, wooden or ceramic silverware. Pictures and posters, especially that of warm places should surround dining room

Beverage

Bullshots

Music

New Orleans Jazz

Osso Buco Milanese

Sensuousness

Osso Buco appeals to the sense of taste and sight; but, it is also the sense of travel far away, the feeling of being in Milan, Rome, and Tuscany. Osso Buco has the magic of transporting you to these cities of Italy; close your eyes, roll the tender meat in your mouth, savor each morsel. Pick the marrow out of the bones with a narrow fork and there is Italy as Italy should be. Osso Buco to me brings back a very good short but splendid time in Milan, sitting in an outdoor cafe, sipping wine, eating pastry. But, somehow, every time I think of Milan, I think of Osso Buco

Ingredients

3 veal shanks

3 Tbls olive oil

1 carrot, finely chopped

1 stalk, finely chopped

1 med onion, finely chopped

1/2 cup white wine

1/2 tsp salt

1/2 tsp pepper

16 oz tomato sauce

1 tsp grated lemon rind

1/4 cup flour

Preparation

Roll veal lightly in flour and brown lightly in hot oil for about 10 mins. on each side. Add vegetables and continue browning until meat is colored and vegetables are soft. Wet with wine a little at a time and let wine evaporate. Add salt, pepper, and tomato sauce. Simmer 1 hour. Add lemon rind, simmer 30 more minutes. Place veal on a platter. Put sauce in a gravy boat.

Accompaniment

Plain Risotto made with chicken broth and aborio rice. Carrots and peas also go nicely, as well as broccoli rabe sauteed in oil.

Table Setting

White lace tablecloth, oversize wine goblets, a mask and a leather outfit to eat dinner in

Beverage

A chilled Olivieto

Music

Verdi's Aida

Philadelphia Beef Stew

Sensuousness

I created this dish in 1976 for the Bicentennial. My wife Sonia and I were in Philadelphia. We were walking through the streets, and there was a mummer's parade going on. It was unfortunately the time of bad things in Philadelphia and I wanted a dish created to honor Philadelphia with all the heritage of the United States that we have from this city. The city no longer closes up at 8 o'clock at night, it is a lively city with a marvelous waterfront. In 1976, we went to Bookbinders and we walked the romantic harborside. My wife spent four years in college outside of Philadelphia and as we walked through the city, thoughts of my wife as a student ran through me. I felt like a whole city was a part of us and that Philadelphia existed for two lovers.

Ingredients

2 lbs boneless chuck

1/4 cup flour

3 Tbls corn oil

8 oz tomato sauce

3 cups boiling water

1 large onion, chopped

1 clove garlic, finely minced

3 whole cloves

1/2 bay leaf

2 tsps salt

1/4 tsp pepper

6 potatoes, peeled and quartered

6 carrots, scraped and cut into 1 inch pieces

12 pearly onions

8 oz fresh peas

Preparation

Dust meat in flour in a paper bag. Brown meat on all sides in a skillet. Take meat out and drain on paper towels. Remove the fat in pan. Put meat back in pan. Add tomato sauce, boiling water, chopped onion, garlic, cloves, bay leaf, salt, and pepper. Cover tightly. Bring to boiling, reduce heat, and simmer 1 1/2 hours. Add vegetables, cover, and simmer 30 mins. Add peas and stir for about 3 mins.

Table Setting

Rustic, dress in costumes for this, be frivolous; if you have an old Benjamin Franklin hat or granny glasses, wear them. This is a recipe that should be conjuring up memories of the 1700's.

Beverage

Hearty Burgundy

Music

Mummer's Records

ENSAMRÄTT: FILM-A:B. LE MAT-METRO-GOLDWYN, STOCKHOLM

Chapter Four

Sensuous People

As I have said the two most important people in my life are my wife, Sonia, and my sister, Patricia. However, through the course of our lives we touch and are touched by many different people. We go through professional, personal, sexual changes in our lives. It is rare for a person to have just one relationship his or her whole life. We have our parents, our schoolmates, dates, lovers, bosses, professors, advisors, mentors, and just so many different types of relationship they are hard to enumerate. The most important part of a relationship is that it should not be forgotten. Lovers, friends, bosses, and associates will come and go but each time we develop one of these relationships we are enriched in some way.

It is hard in the restraints of writing a book to dedicate a recipe to all the people who touched my life; however, in the next 20 pages are recipes that made me associate the food with certain people. These people that came to my mind are not necessarily the most important people in my life, but when I was writing "Sensuous Cooking" they came to my mind.

When you, my readers, make these dishes think of a person who can be reminded by the dish. Dedicate one of our own dishes to a person or persons who have made you more sensual.

84

Caesar Salad a Pattie

Sensuousness

Pattie is my sister. I sort of raised Pattie and in turn was raised also. She is a warm person who loves cats, dogs and homeless things. A big hearted person and one I am proud of.

Ingredients

1 egg

1 Tbl Worcestershire sauce

1 Tbl dijon mustard

2 cloves garlic, minced

Juice of 1 lemon

2 flat anchovies, mashed

3/4 cup olive oil

1 head romaine lettuce, washed

1/2 cup shredded Parmesan cheese

6 slices french bread, cubed

4 Tbls olive oil

1/2 lb Gorgonzola cheese in chunks

Preparation

Crack egg in a large bowl, add lemon juice, anchovies, mustard, garlic, and Worcestershire sauce. Slowly pour in the olive oil, whisking very rapidly. When all oil is used up add romaine and Parmesan. Toss lightly.

Heat oil in large skillet, add bread and gently saute. Top each piece of bread with Gorgonzola and toss into salad.

Accompaniment

Cold water (Pattie's favorite drink)

Table Setting

Decorate the dining room with cats

Music

Rod Stewart

Veal Tara

Sensuousness

This recipe I created for a woman I had once met named Tara, her last name now escapes me, and I made this in a lovely penthouse that she had overlooking Central Park. The funny part about her penthouse is that she was paying only $200 a month rent. Uh, so goes New York!

Ingredients

4 banana peppers, sliced

1 med onion, sliced

2 tomatoes, chopped

2 Tbls butter

1 lb veal cutlets

1 tsp salt

1/2 tsp white pepper

3 Tbls chopped fresh dill

1 tsp dried marjoram

Drop of white wine

5 oz chicken broth

1 tsp minced garlic

Preparation

Brown veal in butter over medium heat in a large pan. Remove. Deglaze the pan with white wine. Add vegetables and saute until vegetables are tender. Add chicken broth and spices. Cover and simmer for 1 hour. Return veal to vegetables and return to warm, cooking about 5 mins.

Accompaniment

A mixture of potatoes and red peppers

Table Setting

Something befitting a penthouse apartment, white tablecloths with white linen napkins

Beverage

Taittenger Champagne

Music

Penthouse Serenade

Veal for a Governor

Sensuousness

I created this recipe many, many years ago. In the 1970's. I lived in Brooklyn and my neighbor was Hugh Carey, Governor of the State of New York. He lived on 3rd Street, by the park. He had a flotilla of kids and he had recently lost his wife. He was an outgoing, nice man and I created this dish for him and as I look back I think of Governor Carey and I wonder what Governor Carey is doing now.

Ingredients

1 1/2 lbs veal cutlets, cut for scaloppine

1 tsp salt

1 tsp white pepper

1/4 cup flour

1/4 cup clarified butter

3 oz sherry wine

1/4 cup heavy cream

3/4 cup chicken stock

1 clove garlic, minced

Preparation

Dip veal in flour. Heat butter in moderately heavy pan. Brown veal on both sides. Remove meat. Add wine and stir the drippings. Remove from heat. Add rest of the ingredients and bring to a low boil. Place meat on platter, pour sauce on top of meat.

Accompaniment
Steamed mushrooms and white rice

Table Setting
Political posters. Red, white, blue setting.

Beverage
Guinness Stout

Music
Irish Folksongs

Mrs. Brown's Wine Steak

Sensuousness

The senses that Mrs. Brown's Wine Steak appeals to is the sense of love and appreciation for old friends. The image that will come is an image of remembering someone. This dish was created by me in remembrance of a dear old friend, Mrs. Brown, whose first name I forgot, which goes back a long time ago. I always said that I will honor this lady in some way and this is how I have done it. This recipe can be altered by the cook of my book to honor a person that they feel that they would like to make a dish for. The lady who I named this recipe for was a lover of steak, as people were back in the '60's when I had first started cooking and when I decided to write this book she would so be honored.

Ingredients

2 Tbls olive oil

2 lbs round steak, whole

1 clove garlic, minced

2 large green peppers, finely chopped

2 large onions, finely chopped

1/2 lb fresh mushrooms, sliced

1 cup red wine

2 tsps salt

1 tsp fresh ground pepper

1 tsp curry powder

Preparation

Brown steak and garlic in Dutch oven quickly in olive oil on both sides. Remove steak.

Add peppers and onions. Saute until tender, approximately 6 mins. Add mushrooms. Saute for 5 more minutes. Stir in wine, salt, and pepper. Return steak, cover, and simmer over low heat for 30 mins. Add curry and simmer an additional 45 mins.

Remove steak and boil down sauce for approximately 3 mins.

Put steak on platter, slice against the grain, and serve the sauce on the side.

Accompaniment

Many vegetables and potatoes. Red cabbage goes well with this dish.

Table Setting

Enjoy with your closest friend. Use a bright and cheery tablecloth, preferably yellow. The plates should be platters.

Beverage

Dr. Brown's Cel-Ray

Music

Herman's Hermit's: Mrs. Brown You Got a Lovely Daughter

Shoulder Lamb Chops à la Mara Lynn

Sensuousness

Mara Lynn was a love lost. So many years have passed since I saw Mara Lynn. She was my senior prom date and my love at that time. Mara Lynn loved to eat and lamb was her favorite dish. Mara, you were one of the reasons for heightening my senses. Picture valleys, mountains, streams, lakes, a sense of peace, a sense of serenity, a recipe to be shared with your loved one. It is elegant, it is quiet, and it has laughter to it also.

Ingredients

2 shoulder lamb chops, 6 oz each

4 oz tomato sauce

3 Tbls butter

2 Tbls chopped parsley

1 hard boiled egg, sliced

1 tsp salt

1/2 tsp black pepper

Preparation

Heat butter in cast iron skillet and brown chops on both sides. Sprinkle with salt and pepper. Combine tomato sauce and parsley and mix well. Spoon tomato sauce mixture over top of chops and simmer, uncovered, for 40 mins Garnish with hard boiled egg.

Accompaniment   Mixture of rice and peas

Table Setting   Should be quiet as streams. Beige tablecloth, white or brown plates

Beverage   Red Zinfandel

Music   Greek bouzouki

Chicken and Avocado in Cream

Sensuousness

This recipe predates my wife, Sonia, by many years. It is one I created because I love avocados and for a certain person who was also fond of avocados. Back when I cooked this 20 years ago an avocado was a rarity.

Ingredients

1 1/2 lb chicken cutlets

1 Tbls salt

3 Tbls butter

3/4 mushrooms, sliced

3 Tbls brandy

1 1/4 cups heavy cream

1 large ripe avocado, cut into strips

2 shallots, finely chopped

Preparation

Cut each chicken cutlet into strips. Heat butter in a heavy skillet. When butter is very hot, but not brown, add the chicken. Cook over high heat until they've lost that raw look. Remove with a slotted spoon and set aside. To the skillet, add the shallots, mushrooms, and more butter. Cook briefly, stirring. Sprinkle with the brandy. Add the cream and cook down by 1/4 over high heat, cooking for about 8 mins. Add salt to taste. Add the cut avocado and cook gently. Add the chicken to heat throughout.

Accompaniment
Brown rice

Table Setting
I like a Spanish table setting with perhaps pictures of a bull ring on the dining room table.

Beverage
Porter (chilled)

Music
Israeli folk music

Veal Zingara

Sensuousness

You will notice there are not too many veal dishes in my repertoire. These are early dishes in my cooking career. Through the years they have become classics. Veal Zingara brings to my mind a woman that I met in Florida, coming back on the train; her name was Rozzie, and she was very important to me back in that time of my life. I invited her to my home, I made this veal dish and every time I think of the veal dish I think of Rozzie.

Ingredients

6 thin slices veal cutlets

1/8 tsp pepper

1/4 cup butter

1/2 lb fresh mushrooms, thinly sliced

3/4 cup heavy cream

1/2 cup cold water

1/4 cup sherry wine

1 Tbls cornstarch

Preparation

Sprinkle veal with pepper. Heat butter in heavy skillet. Add veal and fry over high heat for about 2 mins. on each side. Remove. Add mushrooms and saute about 6 mins. Remove. In a bowl, combine cream, water, wine, and cornstarch. Pour in a skillet. Bring to the boil. Cover and simmer 10 mins. Add veal and mushrooms and cook uncovered for 5 mins.

Accompaniment

Belgian carrots double boiled in dark Jamaican rum

Table Setting

Finest silverware, black plates, always black plates with cream sauces, they are magnificent together. Dress elegantly. This is a dish to think of all the fantasies that you want with your lover and also to make sure that your lover is your friend.

Beverage

The best muscadet wine that you can find

Music

Barbra Streisand

Short Ribs Jardiniere

Sensuousness

This is an old recipe of mine that dates back almost to the beginning of my cooking. I first cooked this for a young lady who really loved ribs; ribs were her specialty but she never had short ribs. Ribs back in the 1950's and '60's always were fatty, pork spare ribs. This dish really set her on her toes. It is a sexy dish in its name and presentation.

Ingredients

1/3 cup flour

2 tsps salt

1 tsp pepper

2 lbs lean short ribs

2 Tbls corn oil

1/3 cup hot water

2 tsps horseradish

6 small carrots

4 medium onions, sliced

2 stalks celery

Preparation

Mix flour with salt and pepper. Coat meat in this mixture. Brown meat in hot shortening in Dutch oven. Drain off fat. Add water and horseradish. Cover and simmer 2 hours. Add vegetables and simmer 30 mins. more.

Accompaniment

Hot buttered rice and potatoes. Potatoes and rice make a very nice mixture as used in Iranian cooking. I brown the potatoes with the rice (on to another recipe for that though).

Table Setting

On a picnic table outside or taken on a picnic with you where you might have a burner to heat up the short ribs or in a pot or a steamer. This is a dish that is, again, messy, but is a sharing dish. There is a deep sense of sharing when it's not called a power lunch when your fingers get all greasy with ribs but it is something both of you are doing at one time. It is something to laugh about. Even paint each other's face with your fingertips. Very, very sexy.

Beverage

Iced cold Czechoslovakian Pilsner Beer

Music

Country Joe and the Fish

Chicken for a Chancellor

Sensuousness

This was my own creation back in the early '60's, for a woman whose grandparents were Chancellors in the court of St. James in England.

Ingredients

2 chicken breasts, split

1 med onion, sliced

1 med pepper, sliced

1/2 lb mushrooms, sliced

1 cup red wine

1/2 cup chicken broth

2 Tbls butter

1/8 tsp fresh rosemary

1 clove garlic, minced

1 tsp poultry seasoning

1 tsp salt

1 Tbls cornstarch

Preparation

Season chicken with the spices. Brown chicken in hot butter in heavy pan. Remove. Add the vegetables and saute 5 mins. Add wine and chicken broth. Bring to a boil. Replace chicken, cover, and simmer 45 mins. Remove chicken again. Add cornstarch and stir until thickened.

Accompaniment
Buttered noodles

Table Setting
As elegant as you possibly can make it. Silver, again, black plates.

Beverage
Guinness Stout and beer

Music
Chopin

Savory Meat Sauce

Sensuousness

Back in the '60's when I was a young man I thought I was so hip and cool when it came to cooking. I had the audacity to cook things in meat sauce for an Italian lady I knew. You just don't cook pasta and meat sauces for Italian people when you're not Italian. It came out much better than I expected. She marvelled that a Russian/Pole could cook such a good Italian meat sauce. This has been a staple in my cooking repertoire throughout the years.

Ingredients

1 large onion, chopped

4 cloves garlic, minced

1/4 cup olive oil

1 1/2 lbs ground round

1 - 2 lb can imported Italian plum tomatoes

1 - 6 oz can tomato paste

1/2 cup water

1/2 cup chopped celery

1/4 cup chopped Italian parsley

2 Tbls salt

2 tsps sugar

1 tsp dried basil

1 tsp ground pepper

2 bay leaves

Preparation

Saute onion and garlic in hot oil in a large kettle over low heat. Add meat and break up and brown over medium. Stir in remaining ingredients. Bring to a boil and simmer 3 hours, stirring occasionally.

Accompaniment

The meat sauce, or gravy as some Italian people call it, should be served over pasta

Table Setting

Nothing should be called "everyday" but not your best knives and forks.

Beverage

Homemade red wine

Music

Jerry Vale

Pork Chops Roma

Sensuousness

In my youth I dated this Italian girl, Diane, who really introduced me to Italian culture, her father was from Italy, she spoke Italian fluently as well as English of course, and she was just full of life and fun and proud to be an Italian. This is a recipe that I created for her.

Ingredients

2 large center cut pork chops

1/2 cup sherry

1 tsp oregano

2 tsps salt

1 tsp white pepper

1 Tbls olive oil

2 cups uncooked rice

4 cups chicken stock

1/4 cup sliced stuffed olives

Preparation

Marinate chops in sherry for 2 hours. Drain and reserve sherry. Dust chops with salt, pepper, and oregano. Brown pork in hot oil in a large, heavy Dutch oven. Remove pork chops. Reduce heat. Add rice to the drippings and stir. Add chicken stock and sherry. Stir. Place chops on top. Cover and simmer for 30 mins. Garnish with olives.

Accompaniment
Sauteed escarole

Table Setting
Quiet and reserved, nothing loud, nice candelabra for easy and gentle lighting

Beverage
Cold Ovietto

Music
Diane's favorite was the theme from The Apartment or any Ferrante and Teicher Melody

Shrimps Joyce

Sensuousness

This dish that I made in honor of Joyce Chin who had such a very profound effect on my life, she heightened my awareness and made me into a better person than I was. What she brought for the few times that I had met her was a deep sense of sensitivity and shareness, a caring of other people, and today Joyce Chin is a nurse married to a lawyer and the mother of a little baby.

Ingredients

1 lb jumbo shrimp, peeled and deveined

1 can water chestnuts, sliced

1 med onion, sliced

1/2 cup clam juice

1/2 cup sherry wine

1/3 cup soy sauce

2 Tbls cornstarch

1 tsp minced ginger

2 cloves garlic, finely minced

3 Tbls peanut oil

Preparation

Marinate shrimp for 1 hour in sherry, soy sauce, 1 Tbls cornstarch, and ginger. Heat oil in a wok and quickly stir fry shrimps until pinkish. Add the onions and water chestnuts. Stir fry 2 mins. Combine clam juice and 1 Tbls cornstarch and stir into the shrimp. Add 1/3 cup of marinade and stir well until mixture thickens.

Accompaniment
White rice

Table Setting

I remember taking Joyce to a restaurant in Boston that was very reminiscent of something out of The Great Gatsby. The table setting - 1930 art deco, art deco pictures and calendars. If you have a calendar of the '30's, hang it up on the wall, or of The World's Fair. The table should be set with flowers.

Beverage
Champagne

Music
Peter Frampton

French Fish Chowder

Sensuousness

What one can do when one is a cook and you blackmail your lover into something. It so happened years ago when a woman I was dating loved French Fish Chowder. She said she would do anything for this dish. I'll say no more.

Ingredients

5 lbs fish heads and bones, gills removed

2 cups dry white wine

6 cups water

2 med onions, coarsely chopped

1 bay leaf

2 cloves garlic, unpeeled but split in half

1 tsp dried thyme

3 sprigs parsley

15 black peppercorns

5 med potatoes, peeled and cut into cubes

4 Tbls butter

1 clove garlic, finely minced

2 med onions, finely minced

1 green pepper finely chopped

3 finely chopped leeks

1/2 cup flour

1 pkg saffron

2 lbs flounder fillets

1 lb haddock fillet

1/2 cup heavy cream

Preparation

In a heavy large kettle combine fish bones, water, wine, coarsely chopped onion, bay leaf, split garlic, thyme, parsley, and peppercorns. Simmer, uncovered, 20 mins. Strain and set the broth aside. Meanwhile, prepare the potatoes and let stand in cold water. Heat the butter in a saucepan and add the minced garlic, finely chopped onion, pepper, and leeks. Cook about 7 mins, stirring. Sprinkle with flour. Add the potatoes, saffron, and 6 cups of the fish broth. Bring to a boil. Cut the fish into cubes and add to the chowder. Cook about 6 mins. Add the cream. Take off heat and serve.

Accompaniment
Lusty French Latusin bread

Table Setting
Nautical, I have a fish net tablecloth

Beverage
Dry white wine

Music
Montovani

Linda's Lo Mein

Sensuousness

Linda is a Chinese woman I had the pleasure of knowing in my youth. Linda loved food, music, travel, and living. I almost equate today a love for living with a love for food. People who don't like food, do they also really like the joys that life brings them. Linda was a very vivacious woman/girl who brought, among other things, this recipe for Lo Mein.

Ingredients

1 lb packaged Lo Mein noodles

4 Tbls sesame oil

6 Tbls light soy sauce

6 Tbls dry sherry

4 Tbls miso

2 tsps sugar

2 tsps cornstarch

8 Tbls peanut oil

2 tsps ginger root, finely minced

8 cloves garlic

2 lbs chuck steak, cut into strips

1 cup bean sprouts

5 scallions, chopped

Preparation

Cook Lo Mein noodles in boiling water for 1 min. Drain. Pour cold water over them. Place in a bowl and sprinkle with sesame oil. Refrigerate. In a bowl combine soy sauce, sherry, miso, sugar, and cornstarch. Mix very well. Set aside. In a wok, heat the peanut oil. Stir fry ginger and garlic for 30 secs. Add meat and cook for 3 mins. Add bean sprouts and scallions. Cook for another 1 min. Add noodles and warm them for another 2 mins. Add soy sauce mixture and stir for another 3 mins.

Accompaniment

This dish needs no accompaniment

Table Setting

I like to eat this as casually as possible, even paper plates would be good. This Lo Mein is great for breakfast.

Beverage

Muscatel wine

Music

Theme from The Sand Pebbles

Brut Stuffed Pork Loin

Sensuousness

This recipe brings back fond memories of a time I had in the South, mainly in southern Georgia and northern Florida. I met this wonderful Southern lady there, who made this fabulous pork loin dish for me. Whenever I think of the South, I think of this Brut Stuffed Pork Loin.

Ingredients

1 - 6 lb pork loin

1/4 cup butter

2 cups onion rings

4 cups unpeeled apple slices

2 cups orange segments

1 tsp curry powder

1 - 10 oz jar red currant jam

1 - 6 oz can frozen lemonade

Preparation

Detach the meat from the bone of the loin. Season well with salt and pepper. In a skillet, with butter, saute the onions until golden. Stir in apples and oranges, salt, and curry. Stuff meat with this mixture. Sew up the meat. Put the pork on a rack. Cover stuffing with foil. Roast 2 hours in a 350° oven. In a saucepan, heat lemonade and jelly to bubbly. Baste the pork roast every 1/2 hour with this combination. Serve the excess glaze on the side.

Table Setting

Lots of Southern type flowers, magnolias, daisies, sunflowers, bright tablecloths with bright plates

Beverage

Magnolia wine

Music

Crystal Gayle

Mad Chicken with White Sauce

Sensuousness

This is a recipe from the late Rocky Graziano who I had the pleasure to share the same barber with when I lived in New York City for a short time. Everybody thinks of Rocky as just a Rocky. Actually he was a very romantic man who appreciated food and who had unique ways of cooking food. This is one of the recipes that he had mentioned to me.

Ingredients

1 broiler/fryer chicken, cut in 3 pieces

1/4 lb butter

1/2 cup olive oil

3 tsps salt

2 tsps white pepper

2 med onions, sliced

15 fresh mushrooms, sliced

1 tsp oregano

6 tsps finely minced parsley

3 cloves garlic, finely minced

1/2 cup dry white wine

1/2 cup chicken broth

Preparation

Dry chicken with paper towels. Melt butter over low heat in a heavy pan. Add oil and allow to heat gently. Salt and pepper the chicken. Brown chicken well in butter/olive oil. Remove chicken and set aside, keeping warm. Saute onions and set aside. Add mushrooms, seasoning, garlic, and wine to pan and cook about 3 mins. Add the chicken broth, the chicken, and onions to pan. Simmer, covered, for 45 mins.

Accompaniment

Rocky Graziano liked every type of pasta imaginable, so any type of pasta would be fine

Table Setting

Try to have it from the ring, pictures of fighters, even a little miniature boxing ring on the table. Rocky also liked roses, dandelions, and assorted flowers.

Beverage

Rocky's favorite drink was beer, of which he invented a diet from drinking beer, so any type of beer would go well with this dish.

Music

Theme from Rocky

100

Maryland Lady Crab Cakes

Sensuousness

This starts my recipes of when I had met Sonia. When I met Sonia who I love today more than I did 20 years ago, we took our honeymoon in the Delmarva Peninsula, Delaware, Maryland, Virginia, ending up at Chincoteague, Virginia and driving back to a town called Easton, Maryland. In Easton, Maryland, we dined on perhaps one of the most sumptuous dishes I ever had, Maryland Lady Crab Cakes, which I intend to duplicate for your potential honeymoons.

Ingredients

1 lb lump crab meat, well picked from shells

1 cup seasoned bread crumbs

1 large egg

1/2 cup mayonnaise, preferably homemade

1/2 tsp salt

1 tsp Worcestershire sauce

1 tsp dried mustard powder

4 Tbls butter

Preparation

In a large bowl, mix bread crumbs, egg, mayonnaise, and the seasonings. Add crab meat and mix gently but thoroughly. Form into patties. In a shallow frying pan, melt the butter and brown Crab Cakes 3 mins. on each side.

Accompaniment
Tartar sauce, cole slaw, and potato salad

Table Setting
As Delmarva as can be, pictures of horses and seascapes

Beverage
Beer with a raw oyster in it

Music
Theme from the motion picture Misty, which was set on Chincoteague

Stir Fried Asparagus

Sensuousness

My darling wife criticizes me for not making enough vegetable dishes. This is a vegetable dish that I think is romantic, easy to make, and should only be made in Spring because that is when asparagus is at its best.

Ingredients

2 lbs fresh asparagus

1/2 lb butter

1/2 cup olive oil

1/4 cup lemon juice

2 tsps salt

Preparation

Wash asparagus well. Cut into diagonals. Pat dry. In a large heavy skillet, heat half of the oil and half of the butter. Add half of the asparagus and cook 2 to 3 mins. over high heat. Remove and drain. Add the other parts butter and oil and cook the remaining asparagus. Add the cooked asparagus and cook another 3 mins. Sprinkle with the lemon juice and salt.

Accompaniment
A tomato/avocado salad

Table Setting
Lofty colors, fresh cut flowers

Beverage
A diet drink or seltzer

Music
Theme from Sweet Charity

Chesapeake Crab Meat Salad

Sensuousness

Going back to my honeymoon at the Delmarva Peninsula, the Chesapeake Bay region is really just one of the most romantic places to spend a week or more. This recipe came from a restaurant in Maryland where they had such well spiced boiled crabs. This is one of their crab meat salads.

Ingredients

1 lb crab meat, well picked

2 Tbls fresh lemon juice

5 Tbls mayonnaise

1 tsp salt

1 tsp curry powder

1 tsp cayenne pepper

1/2 head Romaine lettuce

2 tomatoes

1 cucumber

Preparation

Wash the lettuce and get it ice cold. Mix crab meat in a bowl with the spices and mayonnaise and lemon juice. Fold gently. Fold the crab meat onto the lettuce beds and surround with sliced tomatoes and cucumbers.

Accompaniment
Fresh cole slaw or pepper slaw

Table Setting
This is to be outdoors, preferably by the Chesapeake Bay, on a picnic blanket

Beverage
Iced coffee

Music
From your stereo system or portable radio, should be Rolling Stones music

Duck Montmorency

Sensuousness

Duck is Sonia, my wife's, favorite food and I always try to think of recipes that would incorporate duck into them. This is a recipe that goes back to the French Revolutionary War. Duck does not have to be greasy or fatty if you follow this recipe.

Ingredients

1 - 4 lb duck, quartered

1 - 8 oz can bing cherries

1 cup tawny port

4 Tbls sugar

1 large orange

2 Tbls cornstarch

Preparation

Drain can of bing cherries. Place in a medium bowl. Add port and let stand for 4 hours. Wash and dry duck. Prick skin well with a 3 pronged fork. Broil duck, skin side up, about 25 mins. Remove from broiler. Arrange on a baking pan and roast in a preheated 350° oven for 30 mins. Meanwhile, rub the sugar on the skin of the orange (this gets the oils out and gives a great aroma). Squeeze 1/4 cup juice and add cornstarch to it. Stir until smooth. In a saucepan, combine cherries, port, with cornstarch mixture. Cook, stirring constantly. Add sugar. Stir until it dissolves. Stir sauce on the side with the duck.

Accompaniment   Wild rice

Table Setting   Duck plates or figurines

Beverage   Cherry Heering

Music   Robert Goulet

The Duck

Sensuousness

Duck is Sonia's favorite dish. This recipe is one of her favorite dishes that I've been making for years. It is a recipe that comes from a restaurant on Long Island. It is a recipe that was shared with me and I hope to share with you.

Ingredients

1 - 4 lb duck, whole

5 Tbls Kosher salt

6 slices water moistened bread

1/4 cup black seedless raisins

1 Tbls sugar

1 cup sliced pie apples

Preparation

This dish is done in two steps in two days. It is of utmost importance that it is done this way to remove all the fat, a major problem in the cooking of duck. The first step is to rub the skin of the duck with the salt inside and out. Stuff the cavity of the duck with the mixture made by combining bread stuffing and all the other ingredients. Lay the duck flat in a pan and roast for 2 hours at 375º, pouring the fat off every 40 mins., adding a little water to the pan the last time you pour off the fat. Cool, cut the duck in half, and refrigerate. The next day remove from refrigerator and let stand a couple of hours at room temperature. Cook in a 450º oven for 20 mins. or until skin is crisp.

Accompaniment

A mixture of apples, oranges, and raisins, cranberry sauce, and mashed potatoes

Table Setting

As Long Island as possible, even put a bowl of potatoes in the center of the table

Beverage

Dry Sauterne

Music

Billy Joel

Scallops with Tomato and Paprika Sauce

Sensuousness

The scallop is a much maligned shellfish, mainly because the scallops that are being sold today are flavorless. The little scallops that are being passed off as bay scallops are actually calicos with absolutely no flavor to them. For this scallop dish, if you cannot get Long Island or Cape Cod bay scallops use sea scallops cut up. When I have a scallop dish the memory always takes me to Fire Island and to this funky hotel which was one of the first places that I went to with my wife, the hotel is called Flynn's and I believe it is still there.

Ingredients

1 lb bay scallops (real bay scallops)

4 Tbls butter

1/2 tsp salt

1/2 tsp white pepper

1/4 cup brandy

1 cup tomato sauce

1 tsp paprika

1 clove garlic, finely chopped

3 Tbls parsley, finely chopped

6 tsps grated Parmesan cheese

Preparation

Heat 2 Tbls of butter in a skillet. Add the scallops and salt. Cook, shaking the skillet, for 2 mins. Add the brandy and ignite. Cook 1 min. more. Add the tomato sauce, paprika, parsley, garlic, and pepper. Cook 2 mins. more. Spoon the scallops into scallop shells. Dot with butter. Sprinkle with Parmesan and put it under a broiler for about 2 mins.

Accompaniment
Mushrooms and rice

Table Setting
As Long Island and as Great Gatsby as possible, wear for this dish a white dinner jacket with black tie, have a black tablecloth with white plates, real elegance for this dish

Beverage
Dry Champagne

Music
Billie Holiday

Barbecued Shrimps à la Larocca

Sensuousness

I named this dish after a person I worked with for many years named Charles Larocca. Charley was not much of a cook, but, like myself, he tried hard. This is a recipe that he had given me that he found to be impressive, soothing, and easy to make, but yet one that has pizzazz. When making this dish, old lovers should come to mind and maybe a phone call to such old friend whether it be a girl, boy, or couple.

Ingredients

1 lb jumbo shrimp

1/2 cup olive oil

2 Tbls wine vinegar

2 Tbls tomato paste

1 Tbls oregano

1 Tbls finely chopped garlic

1 Tbls parsley

1 tsp salt

1 tsp pepper

Preparation

Clean and devein the shrimps. Mix all the other ingredients and marinate the shrimps for 4 hours, turning every 1/2 hour. Preheat broiler to high. Place shrimps on broiling pan and cook 3 mins. on 1 side and 2 mins. on the other.

Accompaniment
Rice and peas

Table Setting
Reminiscent of old friends - bring out old pictures of people that you know, pictures of your old neighborhood where you grew up, your parents. Talk of the old times, but don't forget the present times.

Music
Frank Sinatra's A Man And His Music

Sonia at Seven

Sensuousness

Seven is a magical time for me. It is at seven a.m. that my Sonia awakens and it is at seven p.m. that she gets home from work. Don't be scared by the major ingredient; sweetbreads are sublime.

Ingredients

1 lb (pan) sweetbreads

3 cups cold water

3 Tbls seasoned flour

1/4 lb butter

1 large portabello mushroom, thinly sliced

1/2 lb fresh peas

1/2 cup brut champagne

1/2 cup heavy cream

Pinch nutmeg

Preparation

Place sweetbreads in kettle, add water and boil 3 mins. Drain refresh under cold water. Place sweetbreads between two plates and weigh down. Put in refrigerator for one (1) hour.

Take sweetbreads out of refrigerator and remove the outer membrane with a sharp knife. Dice the sweetbreads and dip into flour. Melt butter in a heavy skillet and saute sweetbreads 3 mins. on each side. Add mushrooms and saute 4 more mins. Add champagne, cook down by half, add cream and boil down by another half.

Accompaniment   Steamed rice

Table Setting   A picture of your loved one in the center

Beverage   Sweet sherry

Music   Cats

Chapter Five

Sensuous Elegance

The idea of "Sensuous Cooking" is to make every dish you make an elegant extravaganza; however, some of these recipes just cry out for that one moment. These are special- special dishes. Pull out all the stops for these recipes. The ingredients in these recipes are not very expensive, but the inspirations they can arouse!

Creamy Scallops with Mushrooms

Sensuousness

I created this dish in the 1980's when fish was just about coming into its own. Being raised Catholic, I had to eat fish on Fridays. This was always a chore. This recipe was created 11 years ago, and is such a joy. Shellfish, scallops especially, when they are tender and milky can create a very, very seductive mood.

Ingredients

1 lb sea scallops, sliced thin

1/2 tsp beef syrup

1 tsp lemon juice

1 tsp celery salt

2 Tbls flour

3 Tbls butter

3/4 lb mushrooms, sliced

3 Tbls mayonnaise

Preparation

Pour scallops in mixture of beef syrup and lemon juice. Sprinkle with celery salt, pepper, and flour. Cook scallops over medium heat in butter in a medium sized pan for 5 mins. Add mushrooms and cook 5 more minutes. Blend in mayonnaise. Heat without boiling.

Table Setting

Nautical, put fish nets up in your house, bobbing balls that are used to find fish

Beverage

A light sherry

Music

Nautical, sea worthy, Judy Collins' Salute to Whales comes to my mind or what about the actual songs of The Humpback Whales

Oysters Rockefeller

Sensuousness

Everybody knows the old joke about oysters so no more to be said. By the way it does work with this dish.

Ingredients

36 oysters on the half shell (reserve oyster liquor)

1 lb fresh spinach

1 cup finely chopped scallions

1/2 cup finely chopped celery

1/2 cup finely chopped parsley

2 cloves garlic, finely minced

1 - 2 oz can flat anchovies, drained

8 Tbls butter

1 Tbls flour

1/2 cup heavy cream

1 tsp Tabasco

1 Tbls Pernod or Ricard

1/3 cup grated Parmesan

Preparation

Pick over spinach and remove any rough stems. Rinse well and put into a saucepan. Cover and cook until spinach is wilted, cooking very briefly. Drain well. Squeeze the spinach to remove excess moisture. Put in a bowl. Put the scallions, celery, and parsley in a blender and blend. Chop the anchovies and garlic together very finely. Heat 4 Tbls butter in a skillet and add the scallions and celery mixture. Stir about 1 min. Add the anchovy mixture. Cook, stirring, about 1 min. and add the spinach mixture. Stir to blend. Heat 4 Tbls of butter in a saucepan. Add the flour. Blend with a wire whisk. Add the oyster liquor from the shucked oysters and stir vigorously with the whisk. Stir in the cream. Season with Tabasco. Add the spinach and Pernod. Let cool. Spoon this mixture over each oyster. Dust with Parmesan and bake in a 350º oven for 15 mins.

Accompaniment

This is an appetizer dish but a little slice of lemon on the side or orange goes nice

Table Setting

Have pictures of Nelson Rockefeller in your dining room - he deserves this, he went the way of all good people who eat oysters

Beverage

Cynar

Music

Ferrante and Teicher

Spinach and Mushroom Salad

Sensuousness

This is another salad recipe that can be eaten at work or for a light lunch on a weekend or a romantic encounter.

Ingredients

1 lb raw spinach

10 large white mushrooms, sliced

4 slices cooked bacon, crumbled

2 tsps salt

2 tsps freshly ground black pepper

2 Tbls bacon fat

4 Tbls olive oil

1 Tbls white wine vinegar

1 tsp garlic powder

1 tsp mustard powder

1 large tomato, sliced

Preparation

Wash mushrooms and spinach in ice cold water. Drain well and spin dry. Tear spinach into bite sized pieces. Put into a salad bowl. Add sliced mushrooms. Add crumbled bacon on top of greens. Combine all the rest of the ingredients in a bottle except the tomatoes. Shake well and pour over the salad and toss. Add salt and freshly ground black pepper. Toss again. Put the sliced tomatoes on top, a little bit more salt, and a little bit more pepper.

Table Setting

I like to eat salads at work. They are comfortable to eat and fit a working environment. Work does not have to be a horrible setting to eat; a little tablecloth over your desk, a napkin, a nice fork, and a nice knife, even a little wine glass filled with water is a very nice environment.

Beverage

Coffee, tea, or milk

Music

I feel this is a dish to be eaten at work and whatever music is allowed at your place of business

Pork Chops Paella

Sensuousness

I like to put back to back recipes for pork chops because it is a misused cut of meat. It can be excellent, very tender, very romantic. One chop per person, not much mess or fuss in the kitchen, and again very romantic to eat.

Ingredients

2 center pork chops, 1 inch thick

15 oz fresh tomato sauce

1/2 lb mushrooms, sliced

1 cup water

1 Tbls sugar

3/4 cup regular uncooked rice

1/2 lb peas

2 Tbls corn oil

1/2 tsp mustard powder

1 tsp salt

1 tsp pepper

Preparation

Brown chops in oil. Pour off fat. Sprinkle with salt and pepper. Remove and keep warm. To pan, add the tomato sauce, water, sugar, mustard powder. Bring to a boil. Add rice and stir. Arrange chops in rice. Simmer, covered, for 30 mins. Add peas. Cook approximately 10 mins. more.

Accompaniment

This has just about everything, but, a nice avocado and onion and tomato salad goes very nice

Table Setting

Very Spanish, bright reds or yellows, nothing should be dull in the house, Spanish murals if you have them, Goya prints

Beverage

Iced Brandy (Spanish)

Music

Los Lobos

Netherlands Beef Birds

Sensuousness

I don't know where I got this recipe from. It goes back a long time, perhaps to my childhood, because when I cook this recipe I think of school yard play, stickball, three sewerball, something I guess only growing up in the inner city of Brooklyn could you understand these activities. My mother made this dish a long time ago and I attempted to duplicate it.

Ingredients

1 lb boneless round steak

2 tsps salt

1/4 tsp pepper

1/4 tsp dried marjoram

4 small white onions

1/4 cup flour

2 Tbls corn oil

1 - 6 oz can tomato paste

2 cups water

3 Tbls horseradish

Preparation

Pound steak until very, very thin. The steak that you should use should be for braciole. Sprinkle one side with salt, pepper, and marjoram. Place an onion on each steak. Roll up, tying up to secure. Coat meat with flour. Brown in skillet. Drain off fat. Stir in tomato paste, water, and horseradish. Cover and simmer 1 1/2 hours.

Accompaniment

Buttered noodles, fresh peas with pearl onions

Table Setting

A throwback to the '50's, vinyl tablecloth, dress 50ish with tab collars or snap jack shoes

Beverage

Ballantine Beer

Music

Jerry Lee Lewis

Spanish Veal

Sensuousness

This recipe I encountered on one of my trips. Whenever I think of this I think of sunshine, water, islands in the water, boats, and fun. This is a fun dish and should be served with different people; people that you like to talk about trips with or just have pleasant conversations.

Ingredients

1 1/2 lbs boneless veal, cut into cubes

1/4 cup olive oil

1 tsp salt

1 tsp white pepper

1 bay leaf, crumbled

1 clove garlic, minced

1 small onion, minced

1 - 16 oz can Italian plum tomatoes

1 cup water

1 lb cut green beans, par boiled and drained

2 Tbls flour, mixed in 1/2 cup cold water

Preparation

Brown meat well in heavy Dutch oven in hot olive oil. Stir in salt, pepper, bay leaf, garlic, onion, tomatoes, and 1 cup water. Cover tightly and simmer 1 1/4 hours. Add green beans. Heat to boiling. Reduce heat and simmer 5 mins. Stir in flour mixed with water. Heat to boiling, stirring constantly. Boil 1 min. Arrange veal on platter. Slice thinly and serve the sauce on the side.

Accompaniment

Saffron rice and savoy cabbage

Table Setting

Bright, sunny, yellow tablecloths, yellow plates, very intense lighting sort of to give a light therapy effect to the dinner table.

Beverage

Spanish Sherry

Music

Lady of Spain and Grenada

Beef Agnew

Sensuousness

Not being very handsome and not very sexy and not very rich, I tried to meet women in the most extreme circumstances. One of the ways I found of meeting people of the opposite sex was through the protest marches of the '60's and '70's. Today I'm not quite sure that what I'd done was right or would I do it again. I feel my consciousness was raised by these meetings with various people and I met a lot of interesting people; people today I sometimes wonder whether they were good for me, but this is a recipe I created on a demonstration against the former vice president of the United States who happened to be of Greek descent.

Ingredients

1 lb ground lamb

1 small eggplant, sliced

1 small onion, sliced

3 cloves garlic, minced

1/2 lb feta cheese, crumbled

1/3 cup olive oil

Juice of 1 lemon

2 Tbls salt

1 Tbls pepper

Preparation

In one skillet brown the lamb and break up. In a larger, heavy skillet brown eggplant, onion, and garlic in hot olive oil. Sprinkle with salt and pepper and squeeze lemon juice on it. Let vegetables simmer 5 mins. Combine meat and vegetables and let simmer 5 more minutes. Crumble the feta cheese into the mixture. Toss well and simmer 5 more minutes. Serve on a platter.

Accompaniment

Slices of pita bread and hummus on the side

Table Setting

As '60's as possible with dressed in tight pants or pantaloons, toss in a little polyester. Set the table with paper plates to show the poorness of the people and the power to the people and eat it with plastic forks and knives.

Beverage

Metaxa

Music

Arlo Guthrie

Lamb Chops in Orange Sauce

Sensuousness

This recipe makes me think of very sexual and sensual moments in my life. I served this for a woman that I met going to Lake Placid, New York. She lived in Sheepshead Bay on one side of Brooklyn and I lived on the other but I managed to have her come to my house. I made this dish for her and she gave me a little chef's toothpick to remember the lamb and her.

Ingredients

2 large shoulder lamb chops

12 oz can orange concentrate

2 Tbls corn oil

1 tsp salt

1 tsp tarragon

1 tsp onion powder

1 tsp whole cloves

1 tsp ground pepper

Preparation

In a heavy skillet brown chops well on both sides in hot oil. In a bowl combine orange concentrate with all the other spices. When chops are well brown, pour orange sauce over them. Cover and simmer 1 hour.

Accompaniment

Sauteed beets with butter and some of the orange concentrate

Table Setting

I set the table in honor of Sheepshead Bay with a lobster figurine in the center, with big platters to serve the lamb chops on

Beverage

A beverage that I invented, club soda with a dash of Grand Marnier and 1/4 cup white wine; and I call it The Ganzzy

Music

The Brooklyn Bridge

Stuffed Beef Rolls

Sensuousness

Sensuous Cooking is to take you back with your senses to a memory in time. In the 1950's there was a very big restaurant called Tofinetti's in Times Square. Tofinetti's no longer exists and was replaced by Nathan's, and now Nathan's does not exist. Tofinetti's had big, oversized portions of different foods with big cakes in the windows. The food was O.K. but they did have one dish there called Stuffed Beef Rolls which I have tried to duplicate.

Ingredients

2 large cube steaks

Dash salt

Dash pepper

2 1/2 cups day old bread, cubed

1/2 cup water

3 Tbls butter

3 Tbls olive oil

1 clove garlic, minced

8 oz tomato sauce

2 cloves garlic, crushed

Preparation

Sprinkle steaks with salt and pepper. Combine water, butter, and bread. Spread over steaks. Roll steaks and secure with string. Heat garlic in oil in a Dutch oven. Brown steaks over medium heat. Add tomato sauce and cloves of garlic. Bring to a boil. Reduce. Cover and simmer for 40 mins.

Accompaniment

Boiled potatoes with parsley and dill and shredded cabbage

Table Setting

1950ish - pictures of James Dean, posters of Giant, or I like a poster of Baby Doll, Elia Kazan's controversial movie. Keep table setting simple.

Beverage

Beer and Rye

Music

Eddie Fisher

Fiery Hunan Beef

Sensuousness

Now we are getting close to the senses of the '90's. Hunan cooking was virtually unknown in the United States before the '60's. It is a cuisine known for its heat, but yet subtleties, and just like in life a person should have heat and yet be subtle.

Ingredients

1 lb round steak, sliced thin

1/4 cup soy sauce

3 Tbls dry sherry wine

3 Tbls soy oil

1 clove garlic, minced

1 bunch scallions, sliced

1 cup thinly sliced carrots

1 cup thinly sliced celery

1/2 tsp ground ginger

12 oz button mushrooms

1 tsp salt

1 tsp hot pepper flakes

Preparation

Marinate beef in soy sauce, sherry, and garlic for 1 hour. Heat oil in wok until very hot. Add beef and stir fry for 3 mins. Add vegetables and spices. Cook over high heat for 5 mins. Add marinade. Cook another 2 mins.

Accompaniment

White rice and Chinese pancakes

Table Setting

Plates with pandas, even though pandas are Szechuan, they do come into Hunan. Chinese portraits, chop sticks of course, and lacquer plates.

Beverage

Single Malt Scotch

Music

The theme from Carousel

Sausages in White Wine Sauce

Sensuousness

I find sausages besides being phallic symbols, to be very romantic; they're easy to make, they have a lively taste, and they could be made very elegant rather than just sausages and eggs. This reminds me of the first time I was in Italy where I had such a dish and this is my duplication of it.

Ingredients

1 lb country sausages

1 shallot, minced

1 1/2 cups dry white wine

1 Tbls butter

1 Tbls flour

1 tsp thyme

1 tsp rosemary

1 bay leaf

Preparation

Prick skin of sausages and brown well over medium high heat in heavy frying pan. Remove and drain on paper towels. Discard fat. Saute shallot in butter for 30 seconds. Add flour and stir for about 1 min. Add wine and herbs and simmer sauce for 15 mins. Put sausages back in sauce and heat well.

Accompaniment
Lumpy mashed potatoes

Table Setting
Perfect Saturday afternoon luncheon to be eaten in the kitchen

Beverage
Coca Cola

Music
Songs of Patti Lupone

Beef Risotto

Sensuousness

This dish goes back to 1965 when the word risotto was synonymous with rice. Today, as we know, risotto is a separate course that can cost as high as $25 in the more chi chi restaurants. I made Beef Risotto for that woman I mentioned once before, Rozzie and she loved it very much and I kept it in my repertoire throughout the years.

Ingredients

1 Tbls butter	1 tsp dried basil
1 1/2 lbs ground round	1 1/2 cups water
1 onion, sliced	8 oz Italian plum tomatoes, canned
1 tsp minced garlic	8 oz tomato sauce
1 cup aborio rice	1/2 cup sliced, stuffed green olives
2 tsps salt	1/3 cup grated Parmesan

Preparation

Brown meat in butter in Dutch oven leaving it in chunks. Add onion and garlic. Cook until onion is tender. Fold in rice, salt, and basil. Add tomatoes and tomato sauce. Mix. Add water a little at a time, stirring constantly. When all water is mixed into the rice, fold in the olives, and 1/2 of the cheese. Sprinkle the top with the remaining cheese.

Accompaniment
Radicchio and Endive Salad

Table Setting
Italian checkered tablecloth, candle in an old wine bottle

Beverage
Chianti

Music
Theme from The Apartment

Sukiyaki

Sensuousness

There are many variations of Sukiyaki. This dish can really let the imagination run wild - a woman dressing as a geisha, a man putting a bandana on his head, a Samurai sword, silly Japanese bango, Japanese Kabuki music on the side. It is wonderful transporting yourself to the mystic east.

Ingredients

1 1/2 lbs round steak, cut into strips

1 lb mushrooms, sliced thin

1 bunch scallions, chopped

2 stalks celery, sliced thin

2 large onions, thinly sliced

1 - 8 oz can bamboo shoots

3 Tbls sugar

1/3 cup soy sauce

1/2 cup chicken broth

3 cups raw spinach

Preparation

Rub frying pan with piece of fat from the steak. Brown meat in hot fat. Add all ingredients except spinach. Simmer 10 mins. Add spinach. Cook 5 more minutes.

Accompaniment   White rice

Table Setting   Lacquered plates, black platters if you have them with fancy silverware

Beverage   Sake

Music   Kabuki or Madame Butterfly

My Own Filet Mignon en Brochette

Sensuousness

I created this dish to really impress a woman I once knew way back when. Her name was Marjorie, and still is Marjorie; hopefully, she is alive. She loved to eat as much as I did. And, did I love this woman; she was my first love, she was my passion, my life at the time. I thought without Marjorie I would simply die. In my youth, I was not much, probably still I am not, and, I guess, I tried to impress people, and there is nothing more impressive than food.

Ingredients

2 - 3/4 inch filet mignons	1/3 cup beef broth
1/2 lb mushrooms, sliced	1/3 cup red wine
1 large onion, sliced	2 cloves garlic, minced
1 lb asparagus, scraped	4 Tbls butter
3/4 lb french green beans	1 tsp black pepper, coarsely ground

Preparation

Brown filet mignons in butter on both sides until degree of doneness that you desire. Remove filets and set aside and keep warm. Saute onions, mushrooms, and garlic in remaining butter. Add wine and broth. Bring to a boil. Return steaks, cover and coook 5 mins. Add asparagus and beans and simmer 5 more minutes. Remove filet mignons, place on a platter. Place asparagus and green beans on each side of filets. Pour sauce over meat and vegetables.

Accompaniment
Duchess potatoes or baked potatoes

Table Setting
Platters to serve the food on, bubble glasses

Beverage
A hearty Bordeaux

Music
Johnny Mathis

Ritz Blitz Crab

Sensuousness

This is a dish from the Hamptons in Long Island. Pretend you are Jay Gatsby, put on a real air of sophistication and poise. Crash a party in the summer at the Hamptons, the host will never know.

Ingredients

1 lb lump crab meat

1/4 cup mayonnaise

1/4 cup sour cream

1 rib celery, diced

1 small onion, diced

1/4 lb butter

20 Ritz crackers, crumbled

Dash Worcestershire sauce

1 Tbl Dijon mustard

3 Tbls dry sherry

Preparation

Mix crab, mayonnaise, sour cream, celery, and onion.

Melt butter in large skillet and saute crab mixture 3 mins. Add Ritz crackers, sherry, mustard and Worcestershire sauce. Saute 3 mins. more.

Accompaniment
Carrot and celery sticks

Table Setting
Crab plates and cocktail forks

Beverage
Long Island Iced Tea

Music
Grand Funk Railroad

Tuna á Sclafani

Sensuousness

Peter and Steve Scafani own the best fish market in the New York area - Peter's Fish Market in Midland Park, New Jersey. They are also my friends, and to boot are from Brooklyn. My cooking would be lost without Peter's Fish Market.

Ingredients

1 lb tuna steak

3 Tbls Cajun spices

3 Tbls wasabi (Japanese horseradish paste)

3 Tbls soy sauce

3 Tbls extra virgin olive oil

Preparation

Place a cast iron skillet on flame and get skillet white hot. (Make sure you have house ventilated). Coat tuna in spices. Put in skillet 15 seconds on each side. Tuna will be raw in center.

Mix soy, wasabi and olive oil. Put over tuna.

Accompaniment

Sliced Daikon (a large Japanese radish)

Table Setting

Chopsticks and lacquered plates

Beverage

Sake

Music

Jay And The Americans

HERBERT MARSHALL
JEAN ARTHUR

vägen
till hans hjärta

EN COLUMBIAFILM

Chapter Six

Ethnic Sensuousness

It may be fair to say that all the recipes of the United States are based on some other country or land. The recipes incorporated in this chapter are from countries I have never been to. Indian cuisine is so beautifully subtle, India is a country I wish to go to so much. There is a true Mexican recipe in this chapter as well as Hungarian, Polish, and Australian. I do not pretend to be an expert on all ethnic delicacies; however, I have had reindeer meatballs, rattlesnake, elk, bear, and some preparations indigenous to ethnic restaurants. I have had spleen in a Korean restaurant and calves brains in a French restaurant. When you appreciate the cuisines of other countries, you are appreciating the land and its people and the endeavor of its people. The right blend of ethnicity teaches you above the everyday things in life.

This is my most important chapter. The food of the world I feel bring you closer to the world, the land, the people and yourself.

Oriental Pork with Pea Pods

Sensuousness

My first remembrance of dating was when I was about 16. Like all 16 year olds, I had no money and I took this young girl/woman to a Chinese restaurant which I'll never forget because on the menu in the Chinese restaurant were ham sandwiches, chicken salad sandwiches, bacon and eggs, grilled cheese sandwiches. You remember those Chinese restaurants in New York or whatever hometown you were in - they had the dome pots and they served chow mein and chopped suey. Well, when I started cooking, which was shortly after this date, I thought there has got to be more! This is a recipe for Oriental Pork with Pea Pods.

Ingredients

1 1/2 lbs boneless pork, cubed	3/4 lb mushrooms, sliced
3 Tbls peanut oil	8 oz pea pods
2 Tbls soy sauce	1 can water chestnuts
2 Tbls cornstarch	1 tsp salt
2 cloves garlic, minced	1/4 tsp fresh ginger
1 cup water	1/3 cup salted cashews
1 bouillon cube	

Preparation

Combine 1 Tbls oil, 1 Tbls soy sauce, 1 Tbls cornstarch in a bowl. Add meat. Stir to coat. Let stand 30 mins. Heat 2 Tbls oil in a wok until very hot, but not smoking. Add garlic. Stir fry 10 seconds and remove. Add pork and brown well. Add 1/4 cup water, bouillon. Cover. Cook slowly for 45 mins. Add pea pods and mushrooms. Stir well. Cook 2 mins. Add water chestnuts. Cook 1 min. Combine water, salt, 1 Tbls soy sauce, 1 Tbls cornstarch and pour over meat. Stir well until sauce thickens. Add the cashews and serve.

Accompaniment
White rice

Table Setting
If you can get those dome pots, put the Oriental Pork with Pea Pods in the pot and use that as a serving dish. The plates should be white, chopsticks should be the eating implement.

Beverage
Tsing Tsao Beer

Music
Theme from The Inn Of The 6th Happiness

Striped Bass with Champagne Sauce

Sensuousness

Whenever I think of striped bass I think of a real romantic town on the Hudson River called Grandville on the Hudson. It is bucolic. It is everything a Hudson River Valley town should be like. It is by the water and one night when we were in Grandville a severe thunderstorm struck and the bright lights went on.

Ingredients

For striped bass

2 cups fish veloute	3/4 lb mushrooms, thinly sliced	1/2 lemon
3 lbs striped bass fillets	1 cup Brut champagne	2 Tbls butter
5 shallots, chopped	1 cup heavy cream	

For fish veloute

4 Tbls butter	8 Tbls flour	2 cups fish stock

For fish stock

2 lbs bones and heads from non-oily fish	1 cup coarsely chopped celery	1 bay leaf
5 cups water	1 cup coarsely chopped onions	10 peppercorns
2 cups dry white wine	1 tsp dried thyme	

Preparation

For fish veloute: Melt the butter in a saucepan. Add the flour and stir with a wire whisk. Add the fish stock and stir rapidly with the whisk until thick and smooth. Cover and cook over low heat for 45 mins., stirring occasionally.

Grease a baking dish with a tablespoon of butter. Sprinkle the shallots, salt, and pepper over the bottom of the dish. Arrange the fish fillets and scatter the mushrooms over it. Sprinkle lightly with salt and sprinkle with the champagne. Cover fish with wax paper and bring to the boil on top of stove. Place fish in a 350º oven and bake 20 mins. Remove the wax paper and pour liquid into a saucepan. Add the mushrooms to the saucepan and then cook the mixture down. Add the veloute, stir until smooth. Add cream and lemon juice, swirl in a tablespoon of butter.

Accompaniment
Wild rice and Belgian carrots

Table Setting
Try to decorate the dining room with pictures from the Hudson River Valley, I like a basket of apples as a centerpiece, and your most elegant china

Beverage
Hudson Valley wines

Music
Jackie Gleason

Watercress and Mushroom Soup

Sensuousness

This is the first soup I've incorporated in Sensuous Cooking and later it's going to beget a whole cookbook of soups. This is something that I do right and soups are my best type of cooking. An ideal soup starts off with fresh stock and it is such a warm way to go into a meal. This is one of my favorite soups.

Ingredients

1 1/2 lbs mushrooms, chopped

6 Tbls butter

1 tsp lemon juice

2 bunches watercress, washed carefully

1 small onion, coarsely chopped

6 Tbls flour

6 cups homemade chicken stock

Preparation

Melt 5 Tbls butter in a saucepan. Add the mushroom stems and caps. Sprinkle with salt and pepper and lemon juice. Cover closely and cook about 10 mins., stirring occasionally. Drain but reserve the liquid; there should be slightly over 1 cup. Set the drained mushrooms aside. Cut off and reserve the leaves of the watercress. Chop the watercress stems coarsely and set aside. In a heavy kettle melt 2 Tbls of butter and add the onions. Add the chopped watercress stems and stir to wilt. Cook about 2 mins. and sprinkle with flour. Measure out 1 cup of mushrooms and set aside. Add the remainder to the kettle. Add the mushroom liquid and chicken broth, stirring. Simmer 10 mins. Add the mixture to an electric processer and process coarsely. Return the soup to the kettle. Add the cup of reserved mushrooms and watercress leaves. Bring to the boil and serve.

Accompaniment   Garlic croutons

Table Setting   I like a French table setting with a very, very fine tureen to serve the soup out of

Beverage   V-8

Music   Music from Tommy

Smothered Pork Chops

Sensuousness

This recipe is ambiguous. I believe it could trace its origins to Germany; however, Smothered Pork Chops appears on many restaurants' menus that feature Southern type of cooking. I like to think of it in a Southern vein to be eaten on a sunny day perhaps out of doors.

Ingredients

3 Tbls butter

2 Tbls flour

1 Tbls dried mustard

1 tsp salt

1 tsp black pepper

4 - 1 inch pork chops

1 lemon, sliced

1 med onion, sliced

1/2 cup chicken broth

1 large tomato, sliced

Preparation

Combine flour, salt, mustard, and pepper. Sprinkle over pork chops. Brown chops in hot butter over medium heat in a heavy frying pan. Add remaining flour mixture. Arrange lemon slices, then onion slices over pork chops. Stir in the chicken broth, pouring over the chops. Cook over low heat for 20 mins. Add tomato slices, cover, and cook 10 mins.

Accompaniment
Mashed potatoes

Table Setting
Rustic, vinyl tablecloth, eaten outdoors on a picnic table, iced tea type glasses

Beverage
Holsten Beer

Music
Wagner

Veal with Dill Gravy

Sensuousness

Veal and dill throughout the years has been a natural. It's so romantic how an herb can smell and feel; and dill has that appeal to both senses. The sense of touch is so soft and silky and the smell is so vibrant it opens up the imagination as well as the culinary palate.

Ingredients

2 1/2 lbs boneless veal leg, tied

3 Tbls corn oil

1 tsp salt

1 tsp white pepper

1 med onion, chopped

1 cup hot water

1 bay leaf

3 med potatoes, cut in half

4 carrots, cut in pieces

5 Tbls fresh dill, chopped

1/2 cup sour cream

Preparation

Heat oil in a heavy Dutch oven. Brown meat well on all sides. Sprinkle veal with salt and pepper. Add onions and saute until golden. Add water and bay leaf. Cover and simmer 1 1/4 hours. Remove veal. Add vegetables and bring to a boil. Place on top of vegetables. Simmer another 35 mins. Remove veal and vegetables. Fold in sour cream and dill. Blend well.

Accompaniment
Belgian carrots

Table Setting
As elegant as you can make it - white tablecloth, black plates, big candelabra

Beverage
Muscatel

Music
Rachmaninoff

Garlic Chicken

Sensuousness

This recipe I created because of my love of garlic. You mention the word garlic to somebody and they say: "You can't kiss or you really can't be sensuous with garlic on your breath!" However, garlic is really a very mild form of root. Garlic brings zest to oneself, it is not something that should be hidden or mouthwashed afterward. Garlic is very healthy and in this recipe many cloves of garlic are used. If you are still concerned about your breath, eat some parsley afterward!

Ingredients

1 broiler/fryer chicken, cut into 8 parts

2 tsps salt

1 tsp ground pepper

1/3 cup olive oil

30 cloves garlic

2 tsps rosemary

Preparation

Sprinkle chicken with salt and pepper. On high heat, fry chicken until golden in heavy pan with the olive oil. Stir in garlic and rosemary. Saute about 5 more minutes. Arrange chicken over garlic. Cover and simmer 30 mins. At serving discard garlic.

Table Setting

Earthenware plates and kettles, even serve the chicken out of the frying pan

Beverage

White Zinfandel

Music

Rolling Stones

Veal Piquant with Mushroom Sauce

Sensuousness

Veal Piquant with Mushroom Sauce was created to bring about a romantic evening with a woman I had met at an elegant dance. My intentions were to impress her. The recipe goes back 22 years. It proved to be something we both enjoyed. It is a recipe that should not be taken lightly. Veal, back when I first made it was $3 a pound; today it is more precious. It should be savoured, eaten slowly.

Ingredients

2 lbs veal cutlets	1/4 cup butter
2 tsps salt	2 Tbls flour
1 tsp ground ginger	1/2 lb sliced mushrooms
1 tsp white pepper	1/4 cup sour cream
Juice of 1/4 lemon	1 lemon, sliced
2 Tbls beef broth	6 sweet gherkins

Preparation

Combine salt, ginger, pepper, and beef broth. Toss meat in mixture. Brown meat in butter in a heavy skillet a little at a time; add more butter as needed. Cover and cook over low heat for 10 mins. Remove meat. Combine flour, salt, and mushrooms; stir to make a smooth paste. Add to the skillet, stirring constantly until it thickens. Add mushrooms. Stir in sour cream. Heat but do not boil. Place meat on platter. Cover with sauce. Garnish with sliced lemon and gherkins.

Accompaniment
A bouquet of vegetables - cauliflower, peas, carrots, and rice

Table Setting
Understatedness - white plates and silverware

Beverage
Chardonnay

Music
Beethoven's 5th

133

Winter's Chili

Sensuousness

Winter's Chili brings a sense of warmth to the body; it is not a fiery hot dish, but, like a flame that is burning low. Let this stew rekindle the flame and touch the fire with your mouth. This was the first dish I ever cooked.

Ingredients

1 1/2 lbs ground round beef

1 large onion, diced

3/4 lb dried red kidney beans, soaked

1 - 16 oz can of tomato sauce

3 Tbls olive oil

2 cloves garlic, finely minced

1 Tbls salt

2 Tbls chili powder

1 Tbls ground cumin

Preparation

Soak beans overnight in water to cover. Drain the beans. Fill a pot with water to cover the beans and bring to a boil. Lower the heat and gently simmer for approximately 45 mins.

Meanwhile, heat olive oil in heavy kettle and brown the onions and garlic in the olive oil for about 3 mins. Stir in the meat and cook, stirring, until meat loses its raw color, approximately 7 mins. Drain fat from meat, onion, garlic combination. Stir in the tomato sauce, cumin, salt, and chili powder. Gently simmer for approximately 30 mins.

After beans are cooked, drain and mix in with the ground meat and onions. Cook for approximately 10 mins.

Accompaniment

Rice cooked in chicken broth with garlic, onions, and oil

Table Setting

Place on white platter. Use white china (perhaps with some dark patterns to it), simple utensils, wooden candlesticks, dark tablecloth.

Beverage

Dos Equis Beer

Music

Linda Ronstadt

Passioned Fruit

Sensuousness

The fruit is the offspring of the love making by nature. This is a good dish to contemplate nature.

Ingredients

1 pint strawberries, hulled and split

1 pint blueberries, washed

1 papaya, peeled and diced

1 cantaloupe, cut in balls

3 Tbls granulated sugar

1/2 cup ginger liqueur

Preparation

Place fruit in a large bowl. Toss with sugar. Add liqueur and let marinate in the refrigerator 3 hours.

Accompaniment
Thin slices of prosciutto

Table Setting
Under the moon on a blanket

Beverage
Grand Marnier

Music
Theme from Fantasticks

Indian Cucumber Salad

Sensuousness

Cucumbers are sexy food, especially in the summer time. This a dish should be eaten by the pool or a lake on a warm summer day with somebody you love, it is sexy and a very attractive dish.

Ingredients

1 large cucumber

2 Tbls salt

1 Tbls olive oil

1 Tbls sesame oil

1 Tbls wine vinegar

1 tsp sugar

1 tsp curry

1 Tbls soy sauce

1 clove garlic, crushed

Preparation

Shred, peel the cucumber and sprinkle with salt. Let stand for 2 hours. Pour in a strainer. Run under cold water. Drain. Put in a bowl with all the other ingredients. Refrigerate for 2 hours.

Accompaniment
Pita bread, barbecued chicken, hot dogs, barbecued food

Table Setting
A madras blanket, by a pool

Beverage
Iced Jasmine Tea

Music
Sitar Music

Coquilles Saint Jacques Parisian

Sensuousness

This dish I feel really impresses people. It goes back to the turn of the century and it is simply delicious as an appetizer.

Ingredients

1 lb sea scallops, sliced

1 cup dry white wine

1/2 tsp salt

3 Tbls sweet butter

2 Tbls flour

1 cup milk

1/4 cup coarsely chopped mushrooms

5 Tbls grated Swiss cheese

2 Tbls bread crumbs

Preparation

In a large heavy saucepan, combine scallops, wine, salt. Simmer gently for 5 mins. Drain. Set liquids aside. Cut scallops into small pieces. Meanwhile, in a heavy saucepan heat butter. Add flour. Stir in cooking liquid and milk. Cook for 3 mins., stirring occasionally. Add scallops and mushrooms. Cook for 4 mins. Off the fire add Swiss cheese. Fill buttered shells with scallop mixture. Sprinkle with bread crumbs. Dot with butter and broil until top is brown.

Accompaniment

To be served as an appetizer

Table Setting

Parisian, vivid tablecloths, posters of Toulouse Lautrec or Monet

Beverage

Pernod

Music

Victor Borge music

French Potato Salad

Sensuousness

Potato Salad can take on new heights; there is no reason why a potato salad has to be something that is out of a delicatessen with loads of mayonnaise and very little taste. This potato salad will heighten your sense of the potato.

Ingredients

8 yellow golden potatoes

1 tsp salt

1/4 cup white wine vinegar

1/2 cup olive oil

2 Tbls beef consomme

2 Tbls dry white wine

1 Tbls fresh tarragon

1 Tbls parsley

Preparation

Cook potatoes in salted water for 30 mins. Drain. Peel potatoes while warm. Cut into 1/4 inch thick slices. Place potatoes in a salad bowl. In another bowl, mix salt, vinegar, consomme, and wine until salt is dissolved. Add tarragon, parsley, and oil, dripping the oil slowly into the mixture. Mix well. Pour over potatoes and toss gently.

Accompaniment

This goes very well with a cold steak

Table Setting

A picnic setting, a blanket or a redwood table with plastic tablecloth

Beverage

Porter

Music

Charles Aznavour

Carbonade

Sensuousness

These recipes are old French recipes meant to stir moments of your past, if you're 47 years old such as I am. Carbonade, and French Potato Salad, and Coquilles Saint Jacques are an introduction to French cuisine. The French have a joie de vivre, a taste for life. One of my greatest trips was to Paris and the outlying French countryside. The French taste and savor their food; each bite is a piece of romance unto itself. Carbonade is a gusty old dish.

Ingredients

3 lbs boneless pot roast, cut into 1/2 inch thick slices	1/4 cup beef consomme
5 Tbls butter	1 cup light beer
6 med onions, chopped	1 tsp salt
1 tsp flour	1 tsp fresh ground pepper
1 tsp sugar	1 bay leaf

Preparation

In a heavy Dutch oven heat butter until melted. Add meat and cook until brown on both sides. Remove meat and set aside. Add onions to pan and cook until slightly brown. Stir in flour and sugar and cook until brown. Stir in consomme and beer. Bring to a boil. Return meat to pan. Add salt, and pepper, and bay leaf. Cover and simmer 3 hours.

Accompaniment
White Rice

Table Setting
Light linen tablecloth with linen napkins and black plates

Beverage
Pinot Noir

Music
Cole Porter records

Chorizo Stuffed Eye Round

Sensuousness

Chorizo is a sausage that has finally come to its own in the United States given the Latin/Mexican influence that is now upon our country. Chorizo adds spice and zest and taste to a dish, brightens up the day, is different, adds love and feeling.

Ingredients

4 1/2 lb eye round

1 lb Chorizo sausage

3 Tbls peanut oil

1 large onion, chopped

2 carrots, chopped

1 clove finely minced garlic

2 stalks celery, chopped

2 Tbls chili powder

1 Tbls oregano

1 - 35 oz can plum tomatoes

1 cup beef broth

Preparation

Make a hole through the length of the meat and stuff the meat with sausages. Sprinkle meat with salt and pepper and chili powder. Heat the oil and brown meat on all sides. Remove meat. Pour off fat. Return the meat and add all the other ingredients. Bring to a boil. Place meat in oven and bake for 2 hours.

Accompaniment   Saffron rice

Table Setting   Castenets

Beverage   Dos Equis Beer

Music   Theme from Zorro

140

Cumin Rice

Sensuousness

Cumin is sensuality into itself. A spice that's used in Mexican, Indian, Turkish, Arabic cooking, it has a sexy smell and such a beautiful feel to it. Put cumin into stews, and the aromas that come from it will make you feel cosmopolitan and earthy.

Ingredients

2 cups raw rice

4 Tbls butter

1 large green pepper, diced

1 med onion, chopped

2 tsps cumin

4 cups hot chicken broth

Preparation

Heat butter in casserole. Add peppers and onions. Cook until onion is wilted. Add cumin and rice. Stir. Add the broth. Cover. Bring to a boil and then bake about 20 mins.

Accompaniment
Chicken, steak, just about any meats or a vegetable vegetarian dish

Table Setting
Madras tablecloth, red plastic glasses and candles

Beverage
Jasmine tea

Music
Ravi Shankar

Carpetbag Steak

Sensuousness

Carpetbag Steak is a dish my wife and I made on one of my first camping trips. Camping when you're young, well I don't know if 31 is real young, is very romantic, to sleep under the stars is cuddly, to cook on an open fire, to share the cooking, and to trap your own food which you just don't do in cities. The oysters that went into this dish were fished out of a bay in Cheticamp, Nova Scotia.

Ingredients

3 lbs round steak, in one piece*

1 dozen shucked oysters

1 lemon

*Cut a pocket into it

1/4 lb butter

2 tsps chopped parsley

2 tsps salt

Preparation

Fill the pocket of the steak with the oysters. Sprinkle with the lemon juice. Salt the steak. Tie up the pocket and brush with butter that has been melted and broil for 20 mins. - 10 mins. on each side. When done, melt the rest of the butter in a small pan. When butter is nut brown, pour in remaining lemon. Season with salt and chopped parsley and pour over the steak.

Accompaniment

Baked beans with slices of cheddar cheese in it

Table Setting

This was eaten outdoors on a picnic table under the stars with no tablecloth and on paper plates

Beverage

Australian lager beer

Music

Whatever is on a portable radio, and actually the music for this being an Australian dish by nature is Waltzing Matilda

Meat Loaf with Creole Sauce

Sensuousness

Even though I made this dish over 20 years ago, meat loaf has now become a very in, comfort food. The sensuality of meat loaf goes back to Mom's cooking; by the '30's and '40's meat loaf was very prevalent. I enjoyed this dish 20 years ago and recreated it recently and it is just as enjoyable now as it was then.

Ingredients

For meat loaf

2 1/2 lbs ground beef, pork, and veal combined	1 Tbls butter	5 Tbls fresh dill, chopped
1 1/2 cups fine bread crumbs	1 med onion, finely chopped	1 cup heavy cream
1 tsp grated nutmeg	1 clove garlic, finely minced	1 large egg, lightly beaten

For Creole sauce

1 Tbls butter	1/2 lb thinly sliced mushrooms	1/2 cup beef broth
1 large onion, finely chopped	1 dried hot pepper	1 Tbls cornstarch
2 cloves garlic, minced	1 can - 24 oz imported tomatoes	3 Tbls water
1 green pepper, chopped		

Preparation

For meat loaf: Add nutmeg, salt, and bread crumbs to meat. Heat butter, add onion and garlic in a heavy frying pan until brown. Cool, add to the meat. Add herbs, cream, and egg. Mix well with the hands. Put in a loaf pan and bake for 1 hour.

For Creole sauce: Heat butter in casserole. Add onion, garlic, pepper, and mushrooms. Cook, stirring, 5 mins. Add hot pepper, beef broth, and tomatoes. Bring to the boil and simmer 10 mins. Blend the cornstarch in water. Add cornstarch mixture to the tomato mixture. Simmer 5 more minutes. Serve the Creole sauce on the side of the meat loaf.

Accompaniment

Mashed potatoes and peas

Table Setting

Try to get it as into the '50's as possible, pictures of Elvis or Little Anthony and The Imperials, vinyl tablecloth, vinyl backed chairs

Beverage

Milk

Music

Meat Loaf and Elvis mixed

143

Irish Lamb Stew

Sensuousness

I strongly suggest any couple who's in love to beg, borrow, and steal enough money to take a trip to Ireland. Ireland is everything that pictures show it to be. It is green beyond belief. It is romantic. It is tranquil. I don't like to use the word to describe the Irish thatch roof cottages as, well forget the word even, OK, it's just very romantic, and Ireland is just a wonderful place to spend at least two weeks.

Ingredients

3 lbs lamb stew meat

4 cups boiling water

1 bay leaf

3 tsps salt

1 large onion, cut in eighths

4 potatoes, quartered

3 carrots, cut thick

1 large turnip, cut in squares

3 Tbls flour mixed in 6 Tbls cold water

Preparation

Pour boiling water over lamb pieces in a heavy kettle. Add salt, bay leaf, and onion. Return to the boil. Cover and simmer 2 hours. Add vegetables and simmer another 15 to 20 mins. Remove and onions, keeping warm. Combine the cold water and flour to form a paste and pour slowly into the liquid, stirring constantly, until thickened. Put meat on a platter. Cover with the sauce and the potatoes and vegetables.

Accompaniment

More boiled potatoes with butter and perhaps sour cream

Table Setting

As green as possible, green tablecloth, green plates if you have, green colored wine glasses

Beverage

Guinness Stout

Music

The Clancey Brothers

Celebration Steak

Sensuousness

This dish I inherited from Alma Yee and Joyce Chin who I have mentioned in previous recipes. When there is a holiday or special occasion, Celebration Steak is eaten in these Chinese homes. It is a dish that should be shared with many, many people and you can arrange the ingredients by adding more in proportions to the amount of sirloin steak.

Ingredients

2 lb - 1 inch thick sirloin boneless steak

1/2 cup soy sauce

2/3 cup dry sherry

1/3 cup peanut oil

3 tsps salt

2 tsps ground pepper

Romaine lettuce leaves

Cherry tomatoes

Pickles

Preparation

Marinate steak in soy sauce, sherry, and oil in shallow dish for 1 hour on each side in the refrigerator. Preheat broiler to highest setting. Broil steak 6 mins. on each side. Take steak out of broiler. Let cool on table. Slice diagonally and arrange over lettuce. Garnish with tomatoes and pickles. Add salt and pepper.

Accompaniment
Fried Rice and Lo Mein

Table Setting
Your best chinaware and best silverware, dress very elegantly for this dish, a dark suit for a man, a pretty dress for a woman, something lively also and bright. Make this into a party, invite other people to share this with you and enjoy.

Beverage
Ginseng Tea

Music
Soundtrack from Flower Drum Song or The World of Suzie Wong

Bamboo Shrimp

Sensuousness

My friend Alma, the woman of Chinese origin, influenced my cooking greatly. Another person I had the honor to know, Joyce Chin, has also influenced my cooking. I cooked these Chinese recipes for these two women. Today I don't think I would cook ethnic food for people of ethnic origin. But then again back in the '60's and late '50's what did we know?

Ingredients

1 lb med shrimp, cleaned and deveined	1 tsp salt
1/2 lb mushrooms, sliced	1 tsp curry powder
1 small onion, chopped	2 oz dry sherry
3 scallions, minced	1 oz dry vermouth
3 Tbls soy oil	2 dashes orange bitters

Preparation

Heat oil in a wok. Add mushrooms and onions. Cook 3 mins. Add shrimp. Sprinkle with salt and curry. Cook, stirring, until shrimps are pink. Add sherry, vermouth, and bitters. Cook 2 mins. Garnish with scallions.

Accompaniment
Brown rice that's been steamed

Table Setting
Chop sticks, bamboo serving pieces

Beverage
Dry Vermouth mixed with Sweet Vermouth

Music
Kinks

Jollof Rice

Sensuousness

Jollof Rice is a dish that is African in nature. This African cuisine, namely Ethiopian, is not very prevalent in the United States. In New York City there are two Ethiopian restaurants and there are now Senegalese restaurants in Greenwich Village and one that opened in midtown. In Europe, there are a spattering of, if you want to call Morocco African, OK, there is Moroccan cuisine and there are one or two Ghanaian restaurants in England. This recipe, Jollof Rice, was given to me by a young lady who I once knew who served in the Peace Corps in Africa. She is very charming and again like other people I've me through my life one girl I'll never forget and one who I always associate with this dish.

Ingredients

1 broiler chicken, cut up	3 cups water
1 lb chuck, cut into 1 1/2 inch cubes	3 tsps salt
1/4 cup peanut oil	1 tsp cayenne pepper
1 med onion, chopped	1/8 tsp ground black pepper
1 - 6 oz can tomato paste	1 cup uncooked long grain rice

Preparation

Brown chicken and beef in heavy Dutch oven in hot oil. Add onion and cook until onion is tender. Pour off the fat. Add tomato paste, 2 cups of water, salt, cayenne, and black pepper. Simmer, covered, for 1 hour. Remove chicken and keep warm. To remaining ingredients add 1 more cup of water. Bring to a boil. Stir in rice and cook, covered, 20 mins. Arrange chicken over top of the rice.

Accompaniment
Peanuts

Table Setting
Try to arrange masks in the dining room, eat out of the pot, arrange the meat on a platter, eating with the hands is very proper with this dish and very, very sexy

Beverage
Goats milk

Music
If you cannot find African drum music, then the album of Ola Tungie, who was very popular back in the '50's and '60's

Boiled Tongue with Mustard Sauce

Sensuousness

Tongue is one of the foods that hits all the senses. I remember so well when my mother was cooking tongue and she never told me it was tongue. She said we just call it tongue. Then I remember kosher delicatessens and eating tongue on rye. Then I remember eating tongue in a restaurant called Lou Seigel's, where they made it Polynesian. Tongue is such a wonderful meat, really sexy, almost an aphrodisiac.

Ingredients

For tongue

1 - 3 1/2 lb beef tongue	8 whole cloves
1 clove garlic, split	6 whole peppercorns
2 bay leaves	1 tsp mustard seed

For the mustard sauce

2 Tbls dry Coleman mustard	1/4 tsp salt
2 Tbls boiling water	1/2 cup mayonnaise

Preparation

For the tongue: Cover tongue with water in a large pot. Add spices. Bring to the boil. Cover and simmer 3 hours.

For the mustard sauce: In a small bowl, stir dry mustard with water and salt until smooth. Blend in the mayonnaise.

Accompaniment

Cabbage cooked separate from the tongue and boiled potatoes

Table Setting

The table setting for this dish I feel should be one that brings back family memories - pictures of loved ones, dried flowers on the table, paper napkins for tongue and various things to remind you of the past

Beverage

Dr. Brown's Cel-Ray Tonic

Music

Theme from Fiddler on the Roof

Wok Poupou

Sensuousness

I created this dish in honor of my new wok. It is a mass of ingredients and it is a fun dish to have all your friends, relatives go crazy with the ingredients that you have in it. Double and triple it. Use your imagination. As a matter of fact, plagiarize the recipe and use anything you want.

Ingredients

2 chicken cutlets, cut in cubes

3/4 lb lean pork, cut in cubes

3/4 lb whole medium shrimp

1/2 lb mushrooms, sliced

1 can water chestnuts

3 Tbls peanut oil

1 Tbls soy sauce

1 cup chicken stock

2 Tbls cornstarch

1 tsp grated ginger

1 clove garlic, minced

Preparation

Put shrimp in boiling water. Return to boil, drain, and set aside. Marinate the chicken and pork in 1 Tbls of peanut oil, 1 Tbls cornstarch, and 1 Tbls soy sauce for 1 hour. Heat the remaining 2 Tbls peanut oil in wok. Add the garlic. Stir fry 5 seconds and remove. Add meats and brown on all sides in the hot oil. Add the chicken broth and simmer, covered, 1/2 hour. Add shrimp and vegetables. Stir in and bring to the boil. Cook 2 mins. Mix cornstarch with a little water and stir into the broth until thickened. Serve Wok Poupou in an iron cauldron.

Accompaniment
Rice and shredded scallions

Table Setting
Oriental - bright red tablecloth, bright red linens, white plates or black plates, pictures of Great Wall

Beverage
Hot Oolong Tea

Music
Anything your heart desires from loud rock to quiet elevator music

Turkey Breast Miamilanese

Sensuousness

Turkey has always been one of my favorite foods, but then again, all food is one of my favorite foods. The thought of turkey usually, is Thanksgiving, Christmas, Passover, or holidays of celebration, but turkey can also be used in a sensual dinner for two. Today there are turkey cutlets, which I can't tell at times the difference between veal cutlets, much less expensive, and just as good to taste.

Ingredients

4 turkey breast cutlets, pounded

1 egg, slightly beaten with a little water

1/2 cup dry bread crumbs

1/4 cup flour

1/2 lemon, cut in strips

3 Tbls butter

3 Tbls olive oil

1 tsp salt

1 tsp white pepper

Preparation

Dust turkey cutlets with salt and pepper. Then double dip in egg, flour, egg, and bread crumbs. Heat oil and butter in heavy pan and fry 3 mins. on each side. Squeeze lemon on each cutlet and garnish with the lemon strips.

Accompaniment
Tiny boiled potatoes and pearl onions or a side order of pasta ioli

Table Setting
Candles, flowers, plants, cactus, a garden type feeling

Beverage
Champagne

Music
Cy Coleman music

Peking Shrimps

Sensuousness

I have never been to China and I can't think of any country that could be more romantic and exciting than China. So much of today is owed to the history of China. This dish I made in honor of a Chinese woman that I know, a friend of my sister's who is so small and yet can eat so much. This is a dish that I dedicated to her called Peking Shrimp.

Ingredients

1 1/4 lb medium shrimp, cleaned and peeled

1/4 cup water

2 Tbls soy sauce

2 Tbls dry sherry

1 Tbls cornstarch

1 clove garlic, minced

3 Tbls peanut oil

1/4 cup Karo dark syrup

1 small tomato, cut in wedges

1 med green pepper, cut in strips

1/4 tsp ground ginger

Preparation

Combine water, soy sauce, sherry, cornstarch, garlic, syrup, and ginger. Mix well. Heat oil in wok until very hot and cook shrimp about 2 mins. Add sauce and vegetables and boil for about 2 mins.

Accompaniment
White rice and a side order of salted peanuts

Table Setting
Chop sticks. The dish is to be served in a bamboo utensil with Chinese serving spoons and forks.

Beverage
Plum wine

Music
The soundtrack from 55 Days At Peking - horrible movie but great soundtrack

Cornish Hen with Sherry

Sensuousness

This is a dish that I made for some people that were visiting me from California. One of them was at one time my best friend, Larry, who now calls himself Lance. Lance is more romantic than I am. He was never satisfied with his name so he just arbitrarily changed it. He felt being married wasn't cool and he told everybody he lived with this woman. When they came from California, well, I wanted to impress Lance/Larry with my cooking. I think he was impressed even though he yawned a lot.

Ingredients

2 Cornish game hens, split

1 large onion, diced

3/4 lb mushrooms, sliced

3/4 cup chicken stock

1/2 cup dry sherry wine

1 tsp salt

1 tsp ground pepper

1 tsp poultry seasoning

3 Tbls butter

1 tsp curry powder

1 tsp rosemary

Preparation

Dust the split hens with salt, pepper, and poultry seasoning. Brown in heavy casserole in the butter and remove. Add the other ingredients and simmer 3 mins. Add hens, cover, and simmer 45 mins.

Accompaniment

Baked potatoes with sour cream, which was one of Lance's favorite dishes

Table Setting

Pictures of surfers, Polynesian hats

Beverage

For Lance, Single Malt Scotch

Music

Mamas & Papas

Shrimp Nantua

Sensuousness

We are now getting very close in my recipes to when I first met my beautiful wife who I love more today than I did 16 years ago when I met her. She is far more sensuous now than she was 16 years ago and she has made me really come close to my senses. Shrimp Nantua is one of the last recipes from my single days, which I made for a very charming woman that I met out at Montauk Point.

Ingredients

1 lb fresh shrimp, cleaned and deveined

1 lb mushrooms, sliced

4 Tbls butter

1/2 pint heavy cream

2 tsps flour

2 tsps tomato paste

1 tsp salt

1 tsp white pepper

Preparation

Place shrimps in boiling water. When water returns to boil remove shrimps and cool. Simmer in butter for 3 mins. Add mushrooms. Simmer 3 more minutes. Dilute tomato paste with cream. Sprinkle shrimps with flour. Add the cream and tomato paste mixture. Simmer gently until thickened. Season with salt and white pepper.

Accompaniment
Wild rice

Table Setting
Set the table with a sea faring air to it, serve the dish in shells on top of a napkin

Beverage
Dry white Chablis wine

Music
Beatles - Yellow Submarine

Beef Stroganoff

Sensuousness

I am part Russian and I guess like so many people today proud of my heritage. My grandfather came from Moscow and, even though it was not popular in the '50's, when I was growing up, to be Russian, I was always proud of it. In a way it really even helped me to meet people of the opposite sex because it was unique for somebody to be proud that they were Russian. One of the first remembrances I have of cooking for a person was this classic Beef Stroganoff dish.

Ingredients

1 lb sirloin steak, sliced thin	2 Tbls ketchup
1 lb sliced fresh mushrooms	2 cloves garlic, minced
1 med onion, sliced	1 tsp salt
3 Tbls butter	3 Tbls flour
8 oz beef broth	3/4 cup sour cream

Preparation

Cook mushrooms and onions in butter until tender. Remove. Brown meat lightly on both sides. Set aside 1/3 cup beef broth. Add remain beef broth, ketchup, garlic, and salt to pan. Cover and simmer 15 mins. Blend remaining beef broth and flour. Add slowly to the skillet. Add mushrooms and onions. Boil 1 min. Fold in sour cream and serve immediately.

Accompaniment
Buttered noodles and fresh green peas

Table Setting
Jewel-colored glassware and candlesticks, luxurious damask napery

Beverage
Iced vodka

Music
Tschaikovsky is absolutely marvelous with Beef Stroganoff

Mako on a Bed

Sensuousness

The shark is one of the most feared and yet most fascinating creatures on earth. Danger always heightens the senses. However, there is no danger in eating this "Jaws".

Ingredients

1 lb mako steak

3 Tbls olive oil

3 Tbls soy sauce

2 cloves garlic, pressed

3 Tbls tequila

1 bunch arugula, washed

2 Tbls walnut oil

Preparation

Preheat the broiler.

Mix olive oil, soy sauce, garlic, and tequila, and marinate fish 10 minutes on each side. (Never Marinate fish more than a half hour because it will be mushy.) Broil fish 4 mins. on each side.

Place arugula on a platter. Top with the broiled mako and drizzle walnut oil over all.

Accompaniment
Shredded carrots

Table Setting
Have a centerpiece of a shark on the table

Music
Theme from Jaws

Postscript

In conclusion I hope that you have enjoyed my book, and that it brought to you reflections on your life, a little humor, and recipes that are enjoyable and easy to prepare.

I would like to hear your comments and suggestions about "Sensuous Cooking". You can get in touch with me by writing my publisher and I promise all correspondence will be answered.